LOUIS SULLIVAN AND HIS MENTOR, JOHN HERMAN EDELMANN, ARCHITECT

JOHN H. EDELMANN

at age 30.

Photo by J. F. Ryder, Cleveland. *Paul E. Sprague*

LOUIS SULLIVAN AND HIS MENTOR, JOHN HERMAN EDELMANN, ARCHITECT

by

Charles E. Gregersen, AIA, NCARB

authorHOUSE®

AuthorHouse™ LLC
1663 Liberty Drive
Bloomington, IN 47403
www.authorhouse.com
Phone: 1-800-839-8640

Published by AuthorHouse   07/22/2013

ISBN: 978-1-4817-6796-5 (sc)
ISBN: 978-1-4817-6797-2 (e)

Library of Congress Control Number: 2013911462

This book is printed on acid-free paper.

This book is dedicated to the memory of the late
Richard Nickel
who first introduced me to the work of
John Herman Edelmann

and to
Drew Rolik and Paul Sprague
without whose generous assistance and advice
it might not have been possible.

Contents

Contents

PREFACE

Those who have studied the work of Louis Sullivan with any intensity will have come across the name of John Edelmann, a man who Sullivan always said had a greater influence upon him than any other. Yet with the exception of a short summary of the information which professors Donald Egbert and Paul Sprague had gathered about him up to the time of its publication in February 1966 in *A. I. A. Journal* not one of the many authors who have since written about the origins of Sullivan's architecture has made any effort to find out anything more about this man. When Louis Sullivan wrote *The Autobiography of an Idea*, at the very end of his life, he devoted several pages to the influence his friend, John Edelmann, had exerted upon his philosophical outlook during the formative years of his architectural career. Sullivan even suggested that his famous dictum "form follows function," had its origin in Edelmann's theory of "suppressed functions." Although Sullivan recognized Edelmann's abilities as a draftsman, he failed to acknowledge that Edelmann had been a practicing architect; he also avoided any inference that Edelmann may have influenced the development of his own approach to architecture or that Edelmann had once been his employer.

When the first copy of *The Autobiography* was presented to Sullivan, the architect was on his death bed. In architect Irving Pond's review of the book a few months later, his friend wrote,[1]

> ". . . John Edelmann influenced Louis Sullivan along other than purely philosophical lines, though the book does not tell you this; but I have reason to know it. John was a designer as well as a philosopher and the sketches he made during those vividly described hours of converse between the two sunk deep into Louis' consciousness and Louis' ornament of the earlier period was little more than an interpretation of these emanations from John. Away back in 1880 John Edelmann often sketched for me of an evening in my little room, these conventions which he jestingly called 'the Lotus of the Calumet.' I an aspiring young draughtsman was duly impressed though not inoculated. But the forms did fit into some niche in Louis Sullivan's nature and he made them his own."

---

[1]   Irving K Pond, F.A I.A., "Louis Sullivan's 'The Autobiography of an Idea'," *Western Architect*, June 1924, p.68.

By the 1930s, when Hugh Morrison was gathering material for his *Louis Sullivan, Prophet of Modern Architecture*, Pond was one of the few longtime associates of Sullivan still alive who he could question. Relying on a letter from Pond, Morrison said in reference to Sullivan's early ornament,[2]

> "Its origin may be sought in his friendship with John Edelmann . . . That Edelmann had a somewhat romantic flair for the Egyptian we can guess from his giving the name, 'Lotus Club,' to his summer-outing retreat on the Calumet River; certainly his ornament such as that on the stair rails and elevator grilles of the Pullman Building in Chicago (done when a draftsman in S. S. Beman's office) employs Egyptian forms, and although it is less brittle than Sullivan's, there seems little doubt that Edelmann influenced Sullivan considerably during these early years."

Pond knew the elevator grilles and stair rails of the Pullman Building well because he too had been employed by Beman while it was underway, but apparently he knew of no other surviving ornament by Edelmann or he surely would have mentioned it. Having undoubtedly seen the elevator and staircase ornaments first hand (they were destroyed when the building was demolished in 1957 and only a photograph of the stairs survives) Morrison was sufficiently convinced by Pond's view of the origin of Sullivan's early ornament that he made no effort to find further supporting evidence.

Egbert and Sprague's article demonstrated that Edelmann had a profound influence upon the young Sullivan, but at that stage in their research, they were apparently not yet ready to suggest how Edelmann may have affected the development of Sullivan's architecture. In the absence of well documented conclusions on that issue, some historians have since found it easier to dismiss Edelmann entirely as is evident in the following quote from author Robert Twombley's 1986 biography of Sullivan:[3]

> "Returning to Chicago sometime between July 1879 and June 1880, he [Edelmann] set up as an architect in his suburban Oak Park home. There is no indication of his working for Adler before his final departure from town early in 1881. 'Early in 1879,' therefore, when Sullivan claimed to have placed him in Adler's office, Edelmann

---

[2]   Hugh Morrison: *Louis Sullivan, Prophet of Modern Architecture*, 1st edition, p. 59. Letter from Pond to Morrison dated April 30, 1932.

[3]   Robert Twombley, *Louis Sullivan, His Life and Work*, pp. 94-95.

was still horse farming, his partnership with Joseph S. Johnston three years behind him. And by the latter half of 1881, furthermore, which contrary to his memoirs was the earliest Sullivan could have actually joined Adler full time, Edelmann had left the area. Why Sullivan gave Edelmann so much more credit for his success than he deserved remains an enigma."

When Narciso Menocal collaborated with Twombley on another book on Sullivan fourteen years later, Menocal's view of Edelmann was substantially different. He credited Edelmann with strongly influencing Sullivan from 1884 to 1886 but in a very negative way going as far as to say:[4]

"Fortunately for Sullivan, Edelmann, a political activist, left for New York to take part in Henry George's presidential campaign. With his career very much in jeopardy during that fall of 1886, Sullivan had no recourse but to think the problem [of the Chicago Auditorium design] through, alone, and the result is well known: one of the best buildings in American architecture."

Nevertheless, Sullivan's own account of their relationship in *The Autobiography* acknowledges that if anyone set him on the road to becoming one of America's most famous architects, it was John Edelmann. Who then was John Edelmann, and how did he actually influence Louis Sullivan? Was he simply the source of Sullivan's ornament, a man of no consequence, a negative influence who Sullivan was lucky to see the last of before he began his first major work or was he something else? Edelmann's own work never achieved fame, but if we are to understand where Louis Sullivan's architecture came from, we must be able to understand what Sullivan saw in Edelmann and his work that so inspired him. Ever since Morrison's book was published, it has been suggested by some that because Sullivan's earliest buildings were not much different in general character from other American buildings of the 1880s, they are not deserving of in depth analysis, even including that which Morrison himself gave to some of them. Because of the obvious similarity they share with Edelmann's buildings of the period, that view has been applied to his work as well. It is my view, however, and that of several others who are

---

[4]   Robert Twombley & Narciso G. Menocal: *Louis Sullivan, The Poetry of Architecture*, p.91. Menocal incorrectly credits Paul Sprague with the suggestion that Edelmann worked for Adler & Sullivan when the first designs for the Chicago Auditorium were being prepared. In the source Menocal cites, Sprague said only that the suggestion had appeared in Edelmann's obituaries, but he did not say that he agreed with it.

familiar with them that these buildings display ornamental and architectural eccentricities which have a youthful and exuberant naiveté not found elsewhere except later in the work of the famous Catalan eccentric Antoni Gaudi. I, for one, have found these eccentricities to be far more fascinating than Sullivan's sophisticated but otherwise staid mature work. For that reason alone, I believe the early work of both men remains worthy of the attention which it is given here.

My own interest in John Edelmann has its origin in my interest in Louis Sullivan. In 1956, at the age of thirteen, I was taken by one of my aunts to see the centennial exhibition of Sullivan's work at the Art Institute of Chicago. Sometime later at the site of the half demolished Faulkenau row houses on Wabash Avenue, I met Richard Nickel. He was already so hooked on Sullivan that he was working on what he hoped would become a complete illustrated catalog of Sullivan's work. As the years went by, he and I (like some other Sullivan fans he had picked up along the way) often went to demolition sites to retrieve whatever pieces of Sullivan's magnificent ornament we could.

One of these demolition sites was a residence at 1838 S. Michigan Avenue which Nickel had attributed to Sullivan in his supplementary list in the 1956 exhibition catalog. The ornament looked like Sullivan's, but there was something about it that was not quite right. At that point, none of us knew anything about John Edelmann other than what Sullivan had said about him in *The Autobiography*. It was only when Nickel had a chance to see Paul Sprague's research on Edelmann that Nickel also became interested in him and began to think that Edelmann might be the architect of this particular building which by then had already been demolished.

A few weeks prior to his untimely death in April 1972, Nickel had arranged for me to meet Dankmar Adler's granddaughter, Joan Saltzstein. That meeting led to the two of us collaborating on *Dankmar Adler: His Theatres and Auditoriums*, which was published in 1990. While researching that work, it became evident that John Edelmann had played a significant role in several early Adler projects.

In the months that followed Nickel's death some of us who knew him were drawn closer together in part because it was still not clear whether he was dead or alive. Timothy Samuelson (a young man whom Nickel wanted me to meet, because he said he reminded him of me when we first met) had become a good friend of my wife, Barbara, and me a year before. I had met Paul Sprague by accident roughly ten years before while he was trying to find Nickel, who at the time was still on a lengthy European vacation. It was not until after Nickel disappeared that I met him again.

Quite a bit of the research which I undertook with Tim Samuelson's invaluable assistance in preparing *Dankmar Adler: His Theatres and Auditoriums* has been of use in filling out the picture that Egbert and Sprague began. I owe a particular debt, however, to Paul Sprague himself. He has willingly shared with me all the research which he and Egbert had compiled on Edelmann. Because so much of that data depended on family recollections which can often be wrong, he suggested that I verify (using today's technology) as much as I could of the conclusions that he, Egbert, Samuelson and I had come to over the years.

The Internet has made it possible for me to easily come in contact with a number of people who have been very helpful in expanding our knowledge of Edelmann. These include Robert Keiser of the Cleveland Landmarks Commission, who directed me to a number of sources that have proven essential in understanding Edelmann's work in Cleveland, most notably Drew Rolik, a Cleveland area researcher. Drew Rolik became so fascinated with my project that he repeatedly went out of his way to uncover most of what has now come to light about Edelmann's family and his early life. I owe special thanks also to Ann Sindelar, Research Supervisor at the Western Reserve Historical Society in Cleveland who has been extremely patient with me as each new item she found in their collections led to further inquiries. As in the past, Mary Woolever of the Burnham and Ryerson Libraries at the Art Institute of Chicago has gone out of her way to help me find needed illustrations even when they were outside of the Institute's collections. Jenn Whiteman, Archivist of the Christian and Missionary Alliance and Christopher Neville were most helpful in providing material on The Gospel Tabernacle in New York, the last major work, which Edelmann undertook under his own name. I am also indebted to members of the Edelmann family, most notably his grandson John Arnold Edelman and Henry Bruhl who have been most helpful in providing missing details of John Edelmann's personal life that no archive could have ever yielded.

Over the years as I have been working on this project, I have had the good fortune to run ideas past my daughter Ingrid B. Gregersen-Seo, who is also an experienced architect well versed in the ways of the architectural profession. She had already assisted in the editing of my previous books, so when it came time to submit the manuscript for editing, she was the logical choice to take on the project.

Unlike painting and statuary, where appearance is the only criterion of artistic success, buildings come into existence in response to a multitude of factors: available funding, programming, structure, operating systems, public relations image, the personalities of their developers, architects and their consultants to name but a few. Great architecture is more often than not the result of a series of happy accidents. As a practicing architect with almost a half century of professional experience in historic preservation, I have observed that many issues of architectural history remain a source of debate because they are viewed entirely in artistic terms while ignoring these essential factors. It has been my intent, whenever the record is substantive enough to allow it, to view the work of both Edelmann and Sullivan more as "work product" than as mere artistic artifacts. Through that approach, I hope I have been able to settle some of the questions which remain about the origin of Louis Sullivan's architecture.

Throughout the course of this project various documents and photographs, though of value, were determined to not be essential in confirming its conclusions. It is my intention to deposit them in the Burnham Library of the Art Institute of Chicago for the benefit of future researchers.

CHARLES E. GREGERSEN, AIA

CHAPTER 1 - EARLY LIFE AND TRAINING

Louis Sullivan's account in *The Autobiography of an Idea* of his life from the time he met John Edelmann until he was able to claim the title "Architect" as the junior partner in the firm of Adler & Sullivan is so factually distorted and devoid of many significant details that many historians have been perplexed as to why Sullivan would single out Edelmann as his "benefactor," a distinction he gave to no one else, not even Dankmar Adler. One can only speculate as to what Sullivan was thinking about as he wrote this account. It seems obvious that in order to portray himself as a youthful prodigy without any comparable peers, as he does in *The Autobiography*, Sullivan could not easily acknowledge that Edelmann had already been recognized as an architect at the age of twenty-one, a full nine years before Sullivan was able to claim the same distinction at age twenty-six, let alone admit that he had served a two year apprenticeship under Edelmann. After all, even if someone were to take issue with his account, as Irving Pond almost immediately did, wrong dates and forgotten events could always be dismissed as lapses of memory on the part of an elderly author.[5]

It should not be surprising that Edelmann was not twenty-four years old as Sullivan claimed in *The Autobiography*, (suggesting 1849 as the year of his birth) when they first met at the end of 1873.[6] The United States Census for 1900 was the first in which at least the month and year of a person's birth was listed. It states that he was born in October 1852. With the exception of the Census of 1870, where Edelmann was reported as being eighteen years old on June 2 of that year, the census records for 1860 and 1880 (he is not listed in the few records of the 1890 Census that survive) do not dispute that date. However, Mrs. Sonia Clements, Edelmann's daughter, told Donald Egbert that her father was born on September 19, 1852.[7] Since that date is relatively close to that in the Census, it seems reasonable to assume that it is correct. His given name, according to his father's will,[8] was Johan Herman Edelmann. His first name, like that of his father, was later anglicized to John.

---

[5] Irving K Pond, F.A I.A., "Louis Sullivan's 'The Autobiography of an Idea'," *Western Architect*, June 1924.

[6] Louis H. Sullivan, *The Autobiography of an Idea*, p. 206.

[7] This date and its source is recorded in footnote 54, p. 294 of Paul Sprague's doctoral thesis, *The Architectural Ornament of Louis Sullivan and His Chief Draftsmen*, Princeton University, April 1968. Sprague has informed the author that Donald Egbert received this information by letter from Mrs. Clements.

[8] Last will and testament of, "Johann Michael Edelmann," in Cuyahoga County Archives, "Wills & Estates #E1514," provided by Drew Rolik.

Aside from his places of residence and religious affiliation, documented sources provide no direct information about his early life until the year 1869. Nevertheless these sources provide clues from which it seems reasonable to draw specific conclusions about his life prior to that year.

Edelmann's father, John Michael Edelmann (Michael Edelmann, as he was generally known) was born in Erligheim in the district of Besigheim, just north of Stuttgart, in the Kingdom of Wuerttemberg on September 6, 1818.[9] He applied for permission to emigrate from Erligheim to America with his family in August 1851.[10] According to Edelmann's son, the family name was originally Edelmann von Lilienthal, the "von Lilienthal" having been dropped, when they left Germany. He further stated that the reason for their departure was that, "they fled the German revolution [of 1848] not because they thought it would fail but because they, members of the minor nobility, feared it would succeed."[11] Upon arrival, the family settled in Cleveland, Ohio. It may be inferred from the Census of 1860 that he emigrated with his wife, John's mother, the former Sophia Christina Ekstein, who was roughly a year older than him; her daughter by a previous marriage, Hannah Louise (born Johanna Louise Gaeckle) and his mother Louisa, ages 15 and 64 respectively at the time of the Census. The earliest known residence of the family in Cleveland was at 21 Fountain Alley in what was then a multiethnic neighborhood north of the Public Square and just east of the business district, which the Census for 1870 indicates had a good number of Germans in it but was not dominated by them. Perhaps this was where John Edelmann was born. Certainly his younger sister, Louise Sophia, was born there in 1857. On September 7, 1868, Hannah married Jacob Bluim. By 1870, according to the Census of that year, the couple had given birth to a daughter and were living with the other Edelmanns, but the absence of the grandmother's name suggests that she had died. On November 19, 1874 Louise Sophia Edelmann married Fred Koblenzer.

By 1866, the family had moved across town to a working-class neighborhood on Cleveland's West Side, which the Census of 1870 indicates was predominantly German. There they joined the nearby German United Evangelical Protestant Church of the West Side (now the West Side United Church of Christ). At that time the church was affiliated with the German United Evangelical Protestant Church, a denomination noted for its ecumenical views (it was an offshoot of the Prussian Protestant Church, the

---

9   Paul M. Hartman, Detail of Church Records at West Side United Church of Christ, Established 1853, vol. 2, information provided by Drew Rolik.

10   Trudy Schenk & Ruth Froelke, *Wuerttemberg Emigration Index*, vol. I, p. 37.

11   Joseph Carter, Editor, Labor Lobbyist, *The Autobiography of John W. Edelman*, p. 3.

state church which recognized both the Lutheran and Reformed confessions). Throughout the 1870s, the family remained members of this church. That both of Edelmann's sisters were married there and their father was buried from there suggests that the Edelmann family were among its stalwart members. A strong attachment to the faith this church represented might explain Edelmann's obvious fondness for the Gothic, as a specifically Christian style, and ecclesiastical work during the early years of his career.

For roughly the first two decades of his life in America, Michael Edelmann worked as a teamster. In 1870, he went into partnership with his stepson-in-law in a grocery business named Edelmann & Bluim. Michael Edelmann died shortly thereafter on May 31, 1871, leaving all his property to his widow. After his death, John Edelmann appears to have agreed to take his father's place as a partner in the grocery business, a decision he would later have reason to regret. Having moved to Chicago within a few months of his father's death, Edelmann could have contributed nothing to the operation of the business. Presumably this was done to protect his mother's assets from claims of potential creditors while allowing a share of the business' profits to still be funneled to her.[12]

According to his son, John Edelmann apprenticed himself in, "an architect's office at the age of sixteen."[13] This assertion is supported by the Cleveland directories from 1869 through 1871, in which Edelmann is listed as a draftsman living with his parents. The 1870 Census indicates, however, that he had a much more elevated image of himself because not only did he tell the census taker that he was a year older than he actually was, but he also said he was an "Architect." The rudimentary sketches for a large, otherwise unidentified "country house designed in 1869," which he made in Sullivan's *Lotos Club Notebook* (now at the Avery Library of Columbia University) about six years later prove that he already had sufficient skills to make such a claim. This is the earliest known example of Edelmann's work. Although the sketch is very crudely drawn, the precise features of the design are known because he managed to get it published three years later (Pl.1.).[14] His training in architecture must, therefore, have begun even earlier than his son recalled, which further suggests, considering the low status of his father's occupation (in spite of his reputed noble origin) that his formal education did not go beyond

[12] All the information on the death of Michael Edelmann, his business and the marriages of his children has been provided to the author by Drew Rolik after an examination of the records of same in the Cuyahoga County Archives as well as the transcript of the records of the West Side United Church of Christ, previously noted.

[13] Joseph Carter, Editor, *Labor Lobbyist, The Autobiography of John W. Edelman*, p. 3.

[14] *The American Builder and Art Journal* (Chicago) April 1872.

elementary school. Given the pride that Louis Sullivan implied Edelmann had in his German cultural heritage and the heavily German environment he was living in, it would have been natural for him to seek employment and training with a German architect, and until 1872, Alexander Koehler (1831-1895) was the only one with an office in Cleveland. Edelmann definitely worked for Koehler in 1877, but circumstances indicate that the two had probably met much earlier.

In 1866, shortly after the Edelmann family moved to the West Side, Koehler began constructing a new building for the church they belonged to.[15] This church still stands, but modern additions have now left only one side visible. Even though it was not particularly large, the church was so substantial that it took roughly three years to complete and cost the then incredible sum of $40,000, leaving the congregation in debt for many years to come. Stylistically it was of that mixture of Gothic, Italianate and Romanesque forms generally known in America as "Norman," which James Renwick had popularized in his Smithsonian Institution twenty years before. With time, Edelmann would become known not only as an architect, but also as a very experienced builder and sculptor. It is likely that he began his apprenticeship in all these professions while working on this church, as an employee of Koehler.

Koehler had opened his architectural practice in Cleveland in 1863. The only other Germans with architectural training in Cleveland around the time Edelmann would have entered the work force were Frank (Franz) Cudell and his younger brother Adolph. Both had received their professional training in Aachen, Germany.

Frank had emigrated to the United States in 1866. Upon his arrival, he was briefly employed by the Prague born, New York architect Leopold Eidlitz. Eidlitz had been one of the founding members of the American Institute of Architects. He was not only a noted practitioner of the High Victorian Gothic, but as Kathryn Holliday demonstrates in her *Leopold Eidlitz, Architecture and Idealism in the Gilded Age,* Eidlitz was also a very vocal proponent of the German polytechnic system of architectural education (which stressed construction more than the esthetically oriented French system of the École des Beaux Arts). More important for our understanding of the design approaches of Edelmann and Sullivan, is that since the 1850s, he had expounded on an "organic" approach to architecture which he would later describe in detail in

---

[15]   Date on cornerstone. The *Cleveland Daily Leader* of February 11, 1869, the day after the church's dedication, names Koehler as the architect. Further details of the history of the building are in Steven Rowan's 2000 translation of *The Jubilee Edition of the Cleveland Waechter und Anzieger 1902*, pp. 279-280 which confirms these dates.

his *The Nature and Function of Art, More Especially of Architecture*, published both here and in England in 1881.[16] Just as the form of any natural organism is determined by its function and structure, Eidlitz reasoned that the individual spaces of any building must work in harmony with each other like the cells of a living organism if it is to properly perform its function and that its structural system must also be appropriate for that function. For industrial buildings the architect's task could end there. Although Eidlitz expressed no preference for a particular ornamental style whether traditional or modern, he did assert that in those buildings where man's spiritual values required expression (churches, court houses, residences, etc.), it was the duty of the architect to perceive the true nature of those values and express them in harmony with the rest of the building through appropriate ornamental embellishment. The weakness of Eidlitz's approach was that any building designed to so precisely meet a given program could easily become obsolete if changes were later required in that program. Even during the short time Frank spent in his office, he would certainly have been fully exposed to Eidlitz's vociferous views on these subjects.

After Frank Cudell left Eidlitz's employ, he moved to Cleveland to be joined two years later by his brother Adolph. By 1871, Frank had entered into a brief partnership with Koehler.[17] Prior to then, neither brother had himself listed as an architect. Under these circumstances, it seems reasonable to conclude that Edelmann and both brothers worked together as draftsmen in Koehler's office. Nothing in Koehler's own work at the time reveals any knowledge of the High Victorian Gothic, the style Edelmann's earliest works would in part be derived from. Both Cudells, on the other hand, were fully proficient in that style.[18] It is likely, therefore, that Frank and Adolph Cudell exerted a great influence upon the esthetic aspects of Edelmann's architectural

---

[16]   It has erroneously been asserted that this book had little influence in America because it was only published in England. Kathryn Holliday pointed out that John Root, Sullivan's close friend, knew the work. The author has seen a copy of it also published in 1881 by A. C. Armstrong & Son and printed by J. J. Little & Co., both of New York. It had been acquired by James Brite (later of the firm of Brite and Bacon, architects of the Lincoln Memorial) in 1883.

[17]   Steven Rowan (translator), *The Jubilee Edition of the Cleveland Waechter und Anzeiger, 1902*, p. 245. The firm of, "Cudell and Koehler," designed a triumphal arch as part of a celebration in April 1871 of Germany's victory in the Franco-Prussian War.

[18]   Not only was Adolph Cudell's Portland Building in Chicago an excellent example of their Gothic work but Frank Cudell's still extant Franklin Circle Christian Church in Cleveland of 1875 (see photo on page 22 of Erik Johannesen's *Cleveland Architecture 1876-1976*) features the same kind of plate traceried fenestration that Edelmann used throughout the 1870s.

training while the three of them were working for Koehler. Furthermore, those ideas about function and organic architecture (which both Edelmann and Sullivan would later espouse) most certainly had their origin in Eidlitz by way of Frank Cudell.

CHAPTER 2 - TRIUMPHS AND TROUBLES: WORKING AS AN ARCHITECT WITH OTHERS IN CHICAGO AND CLEVELAND 1872-1880

Apparently attracted to Chicago by the need for architects and builders following the Great Fire of October 1871, Edelmann moved there shortly afterward. The destruction caused by the fire was so extensive that most of the city's prominent architects were suddenly overwhelmed with work. Edelmann, a skilled draftsman with practical building experience, could have easily found a position of responsibility in almost any of their offices. By May 1872, he was listed in the Chicago directory as a draftsman working in the office of Burling & Adler, Architects. Edward Burling (1819-1892) had arrived in Chicago from Newburgh, New York in 1843. Like most of the first generation of Chicago architects, he began his career as a builder. Eventually he became prominent both in politics and the Methodist Church. In January 1871, Dankmar Adler (1844-1900) became his junior partner. Adler, the German born son of a prominent Reform Rabbi, had gained substantial engineering experience as a soldier during the Civil War. In time he would develop important political connections in the Republican Party. Therefore, the principals in the firm had all the social connections and professional credentials required to guarantee success.

Like most architects of the day, both principals appear to have regarded themselves primarily as businessmen. That Adler certainly regarded himself as such is confirmed by his claim to have designed only a small number of the firm's projects. He spent most of his time performing the mundane tasks of supervising construction and the production of construction documents.[19] Since neither Burling nor Adler appears to have had anything more than a passing interest in the esthetic aspects of architecture, it was essential for the success of their business to employ someone, like Edelmann, who already had some experience in that regard. Therefore, it is not surprising that Louis Sullivan would later recall that Adler "thought highly of John."[20] That confidence must have been expressed early, because in the short time Edelmann worked for the firm, he was given the responsibility of designing a residence for Eli Bates in Chicago and the design of the architectural treatment of the First Congregational Church in the Chicago suburb of Oak Park.[21]

---

[19] *Autobiography of Dankmar Adler*, unpublished manuscript in the Newberry Library, Chicago.

[20] Louis H. Sullivan, *The Autobiography of an Idea*, p. 253.

[21] Charles E. Gregersen: *Dankmar Adler: His Theatres and Auditoriums*, Plates 11 and 12.

From Edelmann's arrival in Chicago in 1872 through 1875, all of his designs were Gothic, but his interpretation of the style was more subdued than is generally found in contemporary High Victorian Gothic work. Relying primarily on large areas of unpierced wall and the simplification of detail with a minimum amount of carved ornament, he nevertheless sought to achieve strength and masculinity, that style's sought after traits. Capitals barely projected beyond the face of the wall they supported. Plate tracery was generally used instead of the more traditional molded bar tracery for the windows, and transitions in wall plane were more often achieved through battered belt courses than projecting cornices. In every one of Edelmann's Gothic designs he consistently repeats the same pinnacle, rosette, corbelled roof cornice, plate tracery and chimney details.

The first of these Gothic buildings, the Bates residence, was sketched by Edelmann in Sullivan's *Lotos Club Notebook* (Pl.2.). Edelmann's note that it was, "designed in [18]73," and the amount of detail which he thought worth drawing confirms that this building was his work. This house was relatively plain with little except the engaged columns on the chimney, the dormer details and the roof finials to suggest a Gothic influence.

The chimney detail, which Edelmann drew in both plan and elevation, was used again without modification as a finial at the top of the front gable of the First Congregational Church. That as well as the use of other details found on Edelmann's subsequent church designs help confirm Edelmann as the designer of its ornamental details. The overall arrangement of this church, however, was most likely worked out by Adler (who had designed several similar churches during the late 1860s as an employee of Ozia S. Kinney and after the latter's death as a partner with his son in the firm of Kinney & Adler).[22] Its tall spire, also a feature of these Adler designed churches, would seem to further establish a design connection with Adler, since such spires do not appear in any of Edelmann's other church designs. The fact that the church's chief benefactor, James W. Scoville, would remain an Adler client after the dissolution of Burling & Adler would seem to also confirm this connection.

By the spring of 1873, Edelmann had left Burling & Adler to work as foreman in the office of architect William Le Baron Jenney. The only work that can be attributed with certainty to him while he was employed by Jenney is the firm's unsuccessful competition design for a City Hall—County Building in Chicago. Jenney's firm was one among many which had submitted designs in the competition. (Most of these were published in *The Land Owner* in May 1873.) Edelmann was obviously the author of Jenney's

---

[22]   Charles E. Gregersen: *Dankmar Adler: His Theatres and Auditoriums*, p. 2, 34 &37.

submission (Pl.3.) because much of its Clark Street elevation[23] is identical to the sketch Edelmann drew of the LaSalle Street front (on the opposite side of the building) in the *Lotos Club Notebook* roughly two years later. Jenney may have hired him expressly for that purpose because of his obvious skill as a designer of Gothic buildings. Of the published designs, Jenney's was the only Gothic one. Its obvious source, the English architect Alfred Waterhouse's design for the Town Hall in Manchester was noticed by contemporary critics.[24] This design was the largest and most elaborate Edelmann ever produced. A feature which first appears in it that Edelmann would frequently use later was a battered base to visually anchor the building to the ground. Further evidence of Edelmann's authorship is the treatment of the details on the towers which can be found on his various church designs after this project. Edelmann's sketches in the *Lotos Club Notebook* reveal that during the intervening years he had given further thought to this project, perhaps because he was hoping to submit his own design if another competition for the as yet unbuilt building was called for.

Soon after Louis Sullivan arrived in Chicago in November 1873, he sought and received employment as a draftsman in Jenney's office. It was there that he met and established his lifelong friendship with Edelmann. Sullivan had been attracted to Jenney's firm by the Portland Block, its most prominent recent work and the location of its office. A further connection between Edelmann and the Cudells is suggested by Sullivan's discovery that this building had actually been designed by Adolph Cudell, something he undoubtedly learned from Edelmann.[25] Adolph Cudell had moved to Chicago by early 1871, where he was employed as a draftsman by Jenney until early 1872. Therefore, it also seems likely that he had introduced Edelmann to Jenney.

While working in the office of Burling & Adler, Edelmann became acquainted with Joseph S. Johnston (1843-193?). From 1868 through 1871, Johnston had been working on his own in Chicago as an architect. Presumably the Fire put a damper on his own independent practice, and he was forced to seek employment as a draftsman with Burling & Adler. He does not seem to have stayed in their employ long because by the next year, 1873, he was again working on his own as an architect. That construction of Johnston's design for the Moody Tabernacle, as embellished with Edelmann's details, had begun by

---

[23] The orientation of the perspective is confirmed by the inclusion of the Sherman House (the mansarded building at the left edge) which stood on the northwest corner of Clark and Randolph streets.

[24] Thomas Eddy Tallmadge: *Architecture in Old Chicago*. See pages 125-132 for a lengthy discussion of this project and this competition

[25] Louis H. Sullivan, *The Autobiography of an Idea*, p. 202.

September 1873 suggests that Edelmann began working as a design consultant to Johnston while he was still employed by Jenney.[26]

Sullivan referred to Johnston as, "a man . . . who did school work,"[27] and indeed he did. Within a year, in addition to the Moody Tabernacle, he had enough of it to require Edelmann's assistance. By May 1874 at the latest, Johnston had taken him on as his junior partner in the firm of Johnston & Edelmann, Architects.

The firm's first school commission appears to have been the King School (no longer extant) on Chicago's West Side. The Chicago Board of Education was so satisfied with its design that the Ward School, (still extant, 2703 S. Shields Avenue) built in 1874, the Headley School (now a condominium building, 2710 N. Magnolia Avenue), built in 1875, and several others were built according to the same design. Since almost every known design by Edelmann from this period is Gothic, it is most likely that these elegant Italianate buildings were mainly Johnston's work.

Johnston appears to have been an evangelical Protestant. In fact by 1887, he was no longer listing himself in the city directory as an architect at all but as an "evangelist." Presumably it was he who developed the contacts among Chicago's evangelical Protestant circles which led him and Edelmann to become involved in several significant Protestant church projects. At this stage in his life, Edelmann's Protestant religious affiliation and his skills as a Gothicist would have made him an ideal partner for Johnston.

During the years of his partnership with Johnston, Edelmann produced nine designs of which a visual record remains. The Moody Tabernacle (Pl. 4.) and the competition design for the Plymouth Congregational Church of the following year (Pl. 5.) both in Chicago are the only two that were actually published by the firm.[28] It seems reasonable to assume that at the very least their facades were entirely his work, since these buildings clearly resemble the various Gothic designs Edelmann sketched in the *Lotos Club Notebook* around that time and also featured details found on the First Congregational Church. Unlike the churches Edelmann designed for Burling & Adler, which were all of Joliet limestone, these buildings had polychromatic facades of dark brick with large quantities of contrasting stone trim.

Both the Moody Tabernacle and Plymouth Church were quite large. The Moody Tabernacle alone had a seating capacity of 2,200. What these buildings

---

[26]   *Chicago Tribune*, September 7,1873.

[27]   Louis H. Sullivan, *The Autobiography of an Idea*, p. 255.

[28]   Elevations, plans and sections of the Plymouth and Moody churches appear in the May and November 1874 issues respectively of the *New York Sketchbook of Architecture*.

say about Edelmann's standing in the community and his profession at the time is significant. Dwight Moody was already an internationally known evangelist, and the Plymouth Church was the spiritual home of many of Chicago's most prominent citizens. Having been in Chicago for only two years, Edelmann had become the architect of one of Chicago's most well known churches and potentially the architect of another. Sullivan was so enthralled with this success that at the time, he wrote to his brother Albert concerning Edelmann, ". . . his progress in Architecture has filled me with delight . . . he is one of the smartest and most honorable boys I have ever met and you can make up your mind that my reputation as an architect will always be inferior to his."[29]

Suggestive of the possibility that Edelmann had embraced Eidlitz's view of "organic" design is the way in which the facades of both buildings expressed what was going on behind them. While the facade of the Plymouth Church design was little more than a front for its auditorium, the rear wall of that space was exposed to view between two projecting bell towers which also served as stair towers to the auditorium's balcony. Between them, the main entrance was prominently expressed by an expansive arcade. In the Moody Tabernacle a similar expression of the means of vertical access was achieved with three stair towers, the most prominent of which had a similarly arcaded main entrance at its base. The various functions of the building's different floors were also expressed by significant changes in the fenestration at each level.

Edelmann's "Study" in the *Lotos Club Notebook* for a church in the suburb of Englewood (now part of Chicago, Pl. 6.) was apparently for a commission Johnston & Edelmann were hoping to get in 1875.[30] It is somewhat peculiar because it was to be exceptionally high, although the plan shows that the church was small. The walls were again to have been of brick with stone trim. Only the front elevation is shown in detail. Its principal feature is a large rose window with plate tracery. The capitals and bases of the columns of the front portico are reduced to gently sloped planes, not unlike those which would appear in the work of the Dutch architect H. P. Berlage three decades later. Without knowing how Edelmann planned to treat the other elevations, it is difficult to say whether this was inspired by H. H. Richardson's Romanesque work or was simply another essay in the Gothic.

---

[29] Letter of Louis Sullivan from Paris to his brother Albert of December 7, 1874, quoted in Willard Connely, *Louis Sullivan as He Lived*, p. 63.

[30] The St. Anne Catholic Church and the Swedish Lutheran Bethlehem Church were both begun in Englewood in 1875. Since Johnston was a confirmed Protestant, the former seems an unlikely candidate. No information has been discovered, however, which would link the design to either of them.

In 1875, Edelmann also assisted Burling & Adler on the completion of the St. James Episcopal Church (now Cathedral) and at the same time, the design of the architectural embellishment of their successful competition design for the Sinai Temple (Pl. 7),[31] both in Chicago. This time, however, Adler's confidence in Edelmann may not have been the only reason for using his services. Burling & Adler were then reported as, "having given out the specifications for a considerable number of buildings."[32] They may simply have had too much work to handle on their own.

It may surprise some readers to know that the practice of one architect hiring another to design his buildings was no more unusual then than it is now. (I, for one, have on occasions been hired by other architects to produce designs to meet the requirements of their clients when they were unable to do so themselves.) Early in his career even Sullivan had been shocked to discover that to be the case in Adolph Cudell's design for Jenney's Portland Block. The most well known example of such uncredited work is that of Edelmann's almost exact contemporary, Harvey Ellis (1852-1904). He was easily the most brilliant and farsighted of all late nineteenth century American architects, but his full achievement may never be known because economic circumstances forever placed him at the service of others less gifted than himself.

Edward Burling is credited with the design of the original St. James Church in 1857. Just before the Chicago Fire, his firm had completed an addition to its front consisting of a new narthex with chapel above and a corner tower. The fire left only the tower, the narthex and the south wall of the chapel standing.[33] In the summer of 1872, the commission to rebuild the church was awarded to the Boston firm of Clarke & Faulkner.[34] A photograph of their presentation rendering in the cathedral archives confirms that the exterior walls and roof of that part of the building which now stands to the east of the tower and narthex (less a proposed fleche over the crossing) had been completed in accordance with that design when the project was suspended in late 1873.[35] In early 1875,

---

[31] They were awarded the commission on February 8, 1875. See Charles E. Gregersen: *Dankmar Adler: His Theatres and Auditoriums*, pp. 45-46.

[32] *Chicago Tribune*, May 23. 1875.

[33] See photograph on page 170 of Herman Kogan & Robert Cromie: *The Great Fire, Chicago 1871*.

[34] *Chicago Tribune*, November 24, 1872.

[35] *The Chicago Tribune*, September 7, 1873, April 5,1875. No further work was reported on the building after September 1873. When the pastor gave his farewell sermon in April 1875, he observed that no further work beyond that reported in September 1873 had been done. I am indebted to Richard Seidel who provided me with a copy of the Clarke & Faulkner rendering.

Burling & Adler were retained to complete the building by, "putting a new front," on it and, "refitting the interior."[36]

Burling must certainly have been displeased when a Boston firm was selected to rebuild the structure which had taken him roughly fourteen years of working under the vicissitudes of different pastors and building committees to complete. It is not surprising then, that the only feature of Burling & Adler's new front which might be traced back to Clarke & Faulkner's original design is the large arched window above the center entrance. As if to reestablish his reputation in the public mind as the principal architect of the church, the basic concept of the new front is otherwise very similar to Burling's pre-Fire design. Like any architect who had already been dropped by his client, he was probably not inclined to devote much of his own time to again completing the building. It is not surprising then that the partners would have assigned this project to Edelmann, who had skillfully produced such work for them in the past.

Edelmann's authorship of the decorative elements of this project is confirmed by the presence of his standard vocabulary of Gothic details. By matching the rusticated masonry of the original building, he flawlessly tied the new design into the existing tower and the surviving wall of the former second floor chapel. His "refitting" of the interior was so thorough that even the consoles supporting the truss seats and the cornices at the top of the walls are identical to those he had previously used in the First Congregational Church. However, elements of the roof trusses are likely to have survived from Clarke & Faulkner's work.

The earliest known examples of Edelmann's plastic ornament still survive in excellent condition in and on the church. Their source seems most likely to be found in the published works of the English designer Christopher Dresser. Beginning with the publication of *The Art of Decorative Design* in 1862, Dresser published several well known and well illustrated books on ornament and design. Dresser's designs were also available in the catalogues of the various companies for which he designed products. Unlike Edelmann, whose ornament shows a distinct preference for only one style, the ornaments published by Dresser, like those found in other design manuals of the day, were an eclectic mix inspired by Gothic, Egyptian, Greek, Middle Eastern, Japanese and other sources.

The most elaborate ornaments on the church are the prominent hinges on the exterior face of the front doors (Pl. 36.a.). Their primary motif is a sort of spear shaped leaf that is stubby at its base and elongated on the extended strap

---

[36]   *Chicago Tribune*, May 23, 1875.

of each hinge. In both forms it appears not only in Dresser's publications but also in his manufactured products, particularly those of cast iron.[37] In its stubby form it again appears on the nave side of the casing of the doors leading to the narthex (Pl. 36.b.), but the most interesting of all these ornaments is at the top of the newel posts of the parapet of the organ loft in the south transept (Pl. 36.c.). There, paired modified forms of this leaf face each other in a V-shaped motif that would evolve into the most noticeable motif of Edelmann's later ornament.

For Dankmar Adler, a Reform Jew, the Sinai Temple was a prestigious commission, which he was eager to obtain. That he would seek out Edelmann to assist in providing a suitable architectural treatment for the building again shows the confidence that he still placed in Edelmann's abilities as a designer. Although Adler later referred to the Sinai Temple as one of the few works of the firm for which he was responsible,[38] it clearly has an affinity to Edelmann's other work and there is nothing in Adler's known works that remotely resembles it. Adler's role in this project, therefore, seems to have been to give the building its plan and general form and leave the esthetic aspects to Edelmann as he apparently had done in the First Congregational Church. The front elevation of Edelmann's Cleveland cathedral project in the *Lotos Club Notebook* (Pl. 8.b.) also from 1875 has two towers: each capped by a squared dome with a large plate traceried rose window between them. The obvious similarity between it and the completed synagogue with its large central tower capped by a squared dome flanked by lower squared half domes and a large plate traceried rose window below further support Edelmann's role in the design. All of this evidence is circumstantial, but Edelmann's role in the design is further confirmed by the fact that in 1876 Louis Sullivan, working for Johnston & Edelmann to decorate the interior of their Moody Tabernacle commission at the same time, also decorated the interior of the Sinai Temple.[39]

Although the synagogue did not as a whole have a battered base, the bases of the pilasters at the corners of the central tower had substantial batters. While such Gothic features as the engaged columns and plate tracery were to be found in Edelmann's previous designs, the Gothic pointed arch was only hinted at in this building. This may have been because it was considered inappropriate due to its Christian associations, but it may also indicate, as the "Study" for a church in Englewood might imply, that Edelmann was moving

---

[37] Dresser's designs in various media are extensively illustrated in Widar Halen: *Christopher Dresser, A Pioneer of Modern Design.*

[38] *Autobiography of Dankmar Adler*, unpublished manuscript in the Newberry Library, Chicago.

[39] *Chicago Times*, May 21, 1876; *Daily Inter-Ocean*, June 2, 1876, both quoted in Robert Twombley, *Louis Sullivan, His Life and Work*, pp. 87-89.

away from the Gothic. Whatever the reason, Sinai Temple was the last of Edelmann's works with any Gothic flavor. From then on his approach became increasingly Classically inspired.

As an employee of Johnston & Edelmann, Louis Sullivan had some charge over interior decorative work, but in what other capacities he worked for them can only be conjectured. That he prepared a number of drawings for Edelmann for painted interior decorations from 1874 to 1876[40] for these and possibly other projects and said nothing in *The Autobiography* about work in Jenney's office after Edelmann left suggests that Sullivan began his association with Johnston & Edelmann when the firm was founded, about May 1874. This association continued while Sullivan was in Paris at the École des Beaux Arts during the roughly five months of its 1874-75 academic year and seems to have ended only when the firm was dissolved a year later.[41]

Edelmann's, "Spandrel-Synagogue," sketch (Pl. 37.) in the *Lotos Club Notebook* and the drawings identified specifically for the Sinai Temple by Sullivan are the first drawings that document the cooperation between the two on a particular project.[42] While Edelmann's sketch is the only known detailed drawing of ornament in his hand from the 1870s, it does show the basic characteristics of his ornament at the time. It appears to be for a painted spandrel panel set atop a sculpted plaster arch and cornice. The spandrel itself is filled with foliage. A ribbon cuts across the face of each leaf in a manner common to Dresser's work. The molded plaster face of the arch features the familiar stubby spear shaped leaves facing each other in a repeating V-shaped motif, similar to that seen on the newel post of the St. James organ loft. Sullivan's drawings for this project and others he did for Edelmann around that time feature all of the motifs in Edelmann's sketch, but they lack the flexibility of the original source.[43]

---

[40]   These drawings are illustrated in Paul E. Sprague: *The Drawings of Louis Henry Sullivan* and in Robert Twombley & Narciso G. Menocal: *Louis Sullivan, The Poetry of Architecture*. A number of these, particularly the, "Center-piece in Fresco," in Plate 27 of the latter, are apparently for ceilings of much smaller spaces than could be found in either building. They seem to be for rooms of the type found in expensive residences of the day.

[41]   Sullivan left New York for Paris on July 11, 1874 and was admitted to the École on October 22, 1874. He left it by March 1875 and returned to New York on May 24, 1875. During this period, he prepared at least six drawings for Edelmann. See Robert Twombley, *Louis Sullivan, His Life and Work*, p. 55, 66, 70 and 73 and Drawings 9,11-13, 27 and 28 in Robert Twombley & Narciso G. Menocal: *Louis Sullivan, The Poetry of Architecture*.

[42]   Robert Twombley & Narciso G. Menocal: *Louis Sullivan, The Poetry of Architecture*, plates 40 through 42.

[43]   Robert Twombley & Narciso G. Menocal: *Louis Sullivan, The Poetry of Architecture*, plates 27 through 30, 39 through 42.

Not much is known about Edelmann's design in the *Lotos Club Notebook* for a huge cathedral for the "Diocese of Cleveland." It seems likely that this was a hypothetical project created in response to the division in 1875 of the Episcopal Church in Ohio into two dioceses where the northern half of the state retained the title "Diocese of Ohio" but moved its headquarters from Gambier to Cleveland.[44] That diocese was not, however, ready to build a cathedral until 1901.[45] Edelmann's crudely sketched plan of the building with its ambulatory chapels and long nave is strictly Gothic, but the elevations with their round arches, squared domed towers and the dominant central dome were more in the spirit of the French Romanesque Revival.

The perspective in the *Lotos Club Notebook* of what appears to be a small two story public building with a central clock tower (Pl. 8.a.) may have been for a school or courthouse. Although it cannot be said with certainty, the position of the drawing toward the end of the Notebook on a page with unrelated material from 1876 suggests that this was one of the last drawings Edelmann made in it. Here the tendency toward Classicism was even more pronounced than in the cathedral design. Although traces of the Gothic are still evident in the prominent battered base and steeple, the tall central projecting bay capped by a pediment over a large round arched window, the flanking identical hipped roofed wings and the first floor portico made this a Neo-classic design.

Throughout the years of his partnership with Johnston, Edelmann lived in a boat house in suburban Riverdale seventeen miles south of Chicago's downtown.[46] The boat house was part of an amateur athletic camp known as the Lotos Club, shown on some old maps as a small cluster of similar structures (identified as, "Lotus Place") on the north bank of the Little Calumet River immediately to the west of where the Illinois Central Railroad (now Canadian National) still crosses it. This area is now dominated by heavy industry, but in those days it would have been an idyllic rural retreat. Although Sullivan avoided any reference in *The Autobiography* to his employment during this period by Edelmann or anyone else, he nevertheless discussed at great length his experiences at the club. There the two spent many happy hours discussing philosophy and architecture and participating in athletic events while Edelmann sketched in the *Lotos Club Notebook*.

---

[44]   From: "Episcopalians," in Internet edition of *The Encyclopedia of Cleveland History*.

[45]   Eric Johannesen, *Cleveland Architecture 1876 -1976*, p.88, p.201.

[46]   Louis H. Sullivan, *The Autobiography of an Idea*, pp. 210-213. Directory entries confirm that Edelmann resided in Riverdale throughout the years of his partnership with Johnston.

While discussing the athletic competitions of the Lotos Club in *The Autobiography*, Sullivan, who was only 5'-6" tall,[47] described Edelmann as, "not so very tall . . . huge in bulk and over-muscled," excelling only in feats of strength. The latter is worth noting because of an obvious effort on Edelmann's part to achieve the effect of massive strength in his architecture. Many years later, Edelmann's son would describe his father as a big man between six feet two and six feet three inches tall. This was also confirmed by Edelmann's brother-in-law, Arnold Krimont.[48] Sullivan's phrase, "not so very tall," tells us nothing about Edelmann's stature, but it does suggest that Sullivan was envious of his friend's physique.

As the Sinai Temple was nearing completion in the first half of 1876, Edelmann undertook one last consulting project for Burling & Adler. George B. Carpenter had just engaged them to prepare preliminary designs for his proposed Central Music Hall in Chicago (Pl. 9.). Among Edelmann's miscellaneous architectural details in the *Lotos Club Notebook* are some that are obviously related to this work. A crude perspective of an unidentified facade[49] is almost identical to that of the auditorium wing of the completed building as it faced Randolph Street. A sketch of the top floor of another unidentified building[50] with paired rectangular windows in a smooth faced stone wall is also almost identical to the left end of the Randolph Street front of the office section of the completed building, Immediately below this sketch and intruding partly on it is a sketch of three adjoining round arches resting at the ends on a continuous Tuscan entablature filled with a single row of repeating rosettes. In the completed building, all the arches, both full and segmental, at the fourth floor and the full arches at the sixth floor all rest on continuous entablature courses identical to those shown in this sketch. Since all these sketches are related to the Randolph Street front of the building as built, it is likely Edelmann suggested to Adler, when the project began in 1876, that the functional division into its auditorium and commercial sections be clearly expressed on that front. Nevertheless, from then until he was to again take up the project two years later, Edelmann clearly could have had nothing to do with the various other designs Carpenter said he had worked out with Adler during the interim.[51] The final architectural embellishment of the design may therefore have been affected not only by Edelmann and Adler but other Burling & Adler employees as well. That as a whole the design was a rather

---

47 Information from passport records provide by Timothy Samuelson.
48 Information provided by Paul Sprague.
49 *Lotos Club Notebook*, p. 81.
50 *Lotos Club Notebook*, p. 83.
51 *Chicago Times*, March 2, 1879.

uninspired example of the commercial architecture of the day reinforces this conclusion.

Faced with a lawsuit brought against him by a wholesale grocery firm while he was more or less a silent partner in the firm of Edelmann & Bluim, Edelmann was forced to dissolve his partnership with Johnston and return to Cleveland in the summer of 1876.[52] According to the Cleveland directory of that year, immediately upon his return, he began working as a "clerk" apparently in the grocery business.

By August 1877, the Cleveland directory states that he was working as a draftsman for Alexander Koehler. The only project so far known to have been done by Koehler at that time was the no longer extant Central School in New Philadelphia, Ohio. Construction began in May 1877, and by December of that year, it was substantially complete. This was an eighteen room, three story, mansarded Italianate brick building with elaborate but otherwise conventional Neo-Grec incised ornament on the lintels of all its openings. The absence of anything in its design that might be attributable to Edelmann, suggests that Koehler hired him primarily to supervise its construction.[53]

According to his son, around this time Edelmann began to suffer from epilepsy and decided to try horse breeding in Wisconsin.[54] That he was involved in horse breeding could be true because he was known to be an excellent rider and always very interested in horses. Sullivan, however, believed that Edelmann had been in Iowa working as a farmer.[55] With his widowed mother still living in Cleveland, it is more likely that such events would have taken place closer to home near a rural community like New Philadelphia, where he was just completing a project, than elsewhere. Whatever the truth, this episode in Edelmann's life could not have lasted very long because by August 1878 with the law suit ended and the firm of Edelmann & Bluim dissolved, he had left Cleveland and returned to Chicago

---

[52] Information provided by Drew Rolik from the Cuyahoga County Archives. This suit was filed on September 12, 1876. The surviving records do not show its outcome (it may have been settled out of court) but in it, the plaintiffs claimed they were due $503.58 plus 8% interest, then a significant sum. The debt was not incurred until April 28, 1876. The plaintiffs seem to have been somewhat confused as to who the debtor was. A blank space was left in the complaint for the first name of the Edelmann being sued, and it describes the defendants as, "late partners." There is no way of knowing whether this referred to Edelmann's long deceased father or the dissolution of the firm (which according to the directory of 1876 had been dissolved by August of that year) because only Mrs. Edelmann was listed as running the business.

[53] List of buildings by Alexander Koehler and a short biography as well as a view of the school provided by Robert Keiser of the Cleveland Landmarks Commission.

[54] "In Search of John Edelmann," *A.I.A. Journal*, February 1966, p. 37.

[55] Louis H. Sullivan, *The Autobiography of an Idea*, p. 251.

with his mother, where they took up residence in suburban Harlem (now Forest Park). At the time, this was a heavily German community, like the one they had just come from in Cleveland.[56]

Almost immediately Edelmann was again working for Burling & Adler. Having worked as a consultant on the initial designs for the Central Music Hall, Edelmann's return to Chicago was likely prompted by an offer from Burling & Adler to take charge of the production of its construction documents and perhaps further develop its architectural features.

It was upon his return that Edelmann first introduced Louis Sullivan to Dankmar Adler. Since Willard Connely discovered in the 1950s that Sullivan designed the painted decorations of the Sinai Temple, many of those interested in Sullivan have assumed that this first meeting took place when that project was underway in either 1875 or 1876. Sullivan's account in *The Autobiography* of the first time he met Adler, however, places Edelmann in the Burling and Adler office working as their employee. That could only have happened in 1878 because prior to then, Edelmann only worked for Burling & Adler in 1872, before Sullivan came to Chicago, and the firm ceased to exist at the beginning of 1879. When Sullivan designed the Sinai decorations, he was undoubtedly working as an employee of Johnston and Edelmann, unknown either to Adler or his client. In fact, in 1879 when Sullivan requested an endorsement of his work on the project from the governing body of the synagogue, they tabled it without comment.[57] Presumably they did not know who he was or what he had done.

By May 1878, Edelmann's former partner, Johnston, had been hired by Burling & Adler as an assistant to Burling, who was then acting as Superintendent for construction of the Chicago Customs House.[58] Burling soon found himself accused of incompetence in the performance of his duties on that project, for which he would be indicted in November 1878 and not acquitted until June of the following year. Because the bad publicity generated by the Customs House controversy might threaten the Central Music Hall project, the construction of which was about to begin, it seems likely that its backers forced Burling and Adler to dissolve their partnership. By March 1879, Adler alone had taken sole control of the project. He moved out of the

---

[56] It may be inferred from the absence of both their names in the Cleveland directory, compiled by August 1878, that Edelmann brought his mother with him when he left Cleveland and returned to the Chicago area that year. The Census records for 1880 confirm that Edelmann was living there with his mother and that Germans made up a very significant portion of the community's population.

[57] Irma Strauss, *Adler & Sullivan and the Sinai Temple* (University of Chicago graduate paper) 1974.

[58] The city directory for 1878 describes him as a "mechanic," working on the Customs House project. *Chicago Tribune*, May 25, 1879 confirms that he worked in this capacity under Burling.

office he had shared for years with Burling, and by May 1879, he had moved into a new office which he shared with Johnston, who was again listed in the city directory as an architect.[59] Edelmann also transferred to the new office apparently working for Adler as office foreman and also assisting Johnston with his school work.[60] There he would remain until the Central Music Hall was substantially complete in the beginning of 1880.

There is no reason to doubt Carpenter's attribution of the Central Music Hall design to Adler, but it is highly unlikely that the socially prominent backers of the project (primarily members of Rev. David Swing's Central Church, the building's principle tenant after which it was named) would have considered taking the project to Adler, a German born Jew, rather than to his senior partner, a Protestant of their own class. That Burling, not Adler, first introduced the project to the public by presenting the designs to the owners of the property in December 1878 seems to confirm this conclusion.[61] This is, however, the only time Burling's name was published in connection with the project.

Although Sullivan noted in *The Autobiography* that, "Adler was . . . feeble in design and knew it,"[62] Dankmar Adler's role in the design of the Central Music Hall should not be underestimated. Years later he would refer to it as, "the foundation of whatever professional standing I may have acquired."[63] Over a three year period he spent considerable time on the design of its various features.[64] Although he left its esthetic aspects to others like Edelmann, the building's basic structure and arrangement, including the concept of the two story cast iron store fronts on the State Street side was most likely Adler's. These would leave a lasting legacy in his and Edelmann's work. Here Adler

---

[59] The office is listed as room 21 at 133 LaSalle Street.

[60] Louis H. Sullivan, *The Autobiography of an Idea*, p. 255. While working in the same office with both Adler and Johnston, Edelmann could have assisted Johnston with school work as Sullivan claimed, but Sullivan's claim that Edelmann was also Johnston's partner at this time seems to be in error. Johnston is listed in the directory without any reference to a partner, and Edelmann's name does not appear again in the directory until the following year when he opened his own private practice. Although Johnston had himself listed in the directory of 1887 as an "evangelist," in the Census records of 1900 and 1910 he is again listed as an architect, but by the 1920 Census, he had apparently retired. In the 1930 Census, following the apparent death of his wife Harriet, he and his daughter Mary had left Chicago and moved to Pasadena, California. Since she, rather than her father (who was then 87 years old) is cited as the head of the household, age and ill health had apparently overtaken him. Presumably he died at a very advanced age sometime in the 1930's.

[61] *Chicago Tribune*, December 25, 1878.

[62] Louis H. Sullivan, *The Autobiography of an Idea*, p.255.

[63] *Autobiography of Dankmar Adler*, unpublished manuscript in the Newberry Library, Chicago.

[64] *Chicago Tribune*, March 2, 1879.

sought to provide as much glass show window space as possible while also ensuring that those elements which had to support the loads of the floors would be resistant to fire. To do this, substantial stone piers were placed at the first and second floor levels in line with the main girders to carry their loads and the weight of the masonry walls above. Edelmann's use of an almost identical treatment for the first two floors of two of the buildings he designed in Cleveland three years later, suggests that in the Central Music Hall Edelmann was responsible for the ornamental embellishment of Adler's structural elements.

Sullivan obviously did not want it known that the most critical part of his architectural apprenticeship was the roughly two years he served under Edelmann in the firm of Johnston & Edelmann. Instead *The Autobiography* leaves the impression that he received his professional training at MIT, followed by apprenticeships under Furness and Jenney and finally a lengthy stay in the atelier of Vaudremer at the École des Beaux-Arts in Paris. It is now known that the sum of all that experience was actually little more than a year and a half, far too short for him to have learned anything of substance, as this architect can testify. All he ever said about his subsequent professional experience in *The Autobiography* was that, "His engagements in offices grew longer." The last of these probably not very inspiring "engagements" was with local architect William Strippelman for whom he was working as late as April 4, 1880, the evidence of which he may still have had at hand as he was writing that remark.[65] In reality, Sullivan would serve a total of nine years of architectural apprenticeship, the period of time required by later registration laws for persons (like Sullivan) who had not completed five years of academic training. In short he was not the architectural prodigy he obviously wanted to be remembered as.

By the spring of 1880, Edelmann apparently wanted to again be his own boss. In *The Autobiography*, Sullivan states that Edelmann had several discussions with Adler before finally introducing him as his potential replacement as office foreman. Sullivan erroneously claimed that these events took place as the Central Music Hall was, "nearing completion . . . early in 1879," which we know did not actually happen until a full year later. Sullivan further claimed that he became Adler's junior partner on May 1, 1880.[66] Building reports, drawings and the city directory prove that did not happen

---

65 A red ink sketch by Sullivan on Strippelman's stationary with this date written in Sullivan's hand at the blank provided for same in its red letterhead is in the collections of the Burnham Library of the Art Institute of Chicago.

66 Louis H. Sullivan, *The Autobiography of an Idea*, 255-256.

until May 1882. The timing of Sullivan's employment by Strippelman and Edelmann's departure from Adler's office in the spring of 1880 suggests, however, that he entered Adler's employ on or near May 1, 1880.

Following his remarkably successful design for the Central Music Hall's auditorium, Adler would forever be regarded primarily as the creator of acoustically superior theaters and auditoriums. In the last months Edelmann worked for Adler, it was that reputation alone which led to his firm's first theater commission, the Grand Opera House in Chicago. This theater, built by attorney William Borden, was a rear addition to a building constructed just after the Great Fire. Although it was not completed until months after Edelmann's departure, the permit for it was issued on May 7, 1880[67] too early for Sullivan to have had any effect on the project except for its painted decor, which was undertaken only in the final stages of construction. The working drawings would, therefore, have been completed and submitted for permit before Sullivan entered Adler's employ. A photograph of the proscenium boxes, taken after the theater had been remodeled about a decade later, shows that the original molded plaster ornament was still intact around the proscenium.[68] Since these details would likely have appeared on the drawings when they were taken for permit and are in Edelmann's style, only Edelmann could have been their author.

Throughout the 1870s, Edelmann's use of sculpted ornament played so subordinate a role in his designs that its character is only evident on close inspection of the work. If he had selected a style other than the Dresser-inspired one he obviously preferred, it would have had little overall effect upon his architecture. Even in the interior of such buildings as the Moody Tabernacle and the Central Music Hall the use of sculpted ornament was relatively sparse. That all changed when Edelmann was called upon by Adler to decorate the interior of the Grand Opera House. It is likely that in keeping with his acoustical theories, Adler instructed Edelmann to break up the plaster surfaces of the proscenium as much as possible to prevent sound from reflecting from them.[69] The result was a profusion of high relief ornament that would become characteristic of Edelmann's architecture. The tympanum of the arch above the upper level boxes was arranged like half of one of his plate traceried rose windows, but instead of glass, the circles were filled with sculpted rosettes like those which had first appeared in the Plymouth Church and Sinai Temple designs. With the initial inspiration of Dresser's work far

---

[67] City of Chicago Building Department records.

[68] Reproduced in Charles E. Gregersen: *Dankmar Adler: His Theatres and Auditoriums*, as Plate 23.

[69] Discussed at length in Charles E. Gregersen: *Dankmar Adler: His Theatres and Auditoriums*.

behind him, Edelmann's ornament had evolved into a very personal style. The stylized versions of the Queen Anne sunflower and stalk motif on the piers at either side of the lower level boxes were more likely representations of "the Lotus of the Calumet" (which Edelmann told Irving Pond was the true source of his ornament.)[70] A unique feature which Edelmann would use only once again a few months later was a series of projecting squares with a small recessed rosette at the center of each which ran across the surface of the fascia immediately above the upper level boxes.

The substantial residence which William Borden's father, John Borden, built for himself (Pl. 10.) in suburban Hyde Park (now part of Chicago) is the one Adler commission from 1880 whose authorship has been questioned by some Sullivan devotees. During that year, only one of three people is likely to have been in a position to produce its overall design: Adler himself or one of his two foremen, Edelmann or Sullivan. There can be no doubt that Adler was not its designer. Not only did the building look unlike any that can be otherwise credited to him, he generally had such an aversion to designing private homes that he even had Sullivan design his own in 1885.

Considering what Sullivan said about this project, it is unlikely that it can be attributed to him either. In 1916, with both Adler and Edelmann long dead, Sullivan could easily have taken credit for the building's design without fear of contradiction, but he did not do so. In his 1916 paper "Development of Construction," while referring to the Borden Block as a, "joint venture," between himself and Adler, he merely said that, "we [referring to himself and Adler] built a house [for] John Borden."[71] Having claimed a major design role for himself in the Borden Block, he clearly was not prepared to make such a claim for the Borden Residence. In *The Autobiography*, published eight years later, he distanced himself even further from the project by saying only that "there came into the office . . . a large substantial residence," as if to acknowledge that others in Adler's office had been in charge of it.[72] That construction was not begun until long after Edelmann was again on his own seems to confirm Sullivan's admission to have at least been one of its builders. The elaborate dormer for four third floor windows on the south facade is the only detail which seems alien to the rest of the design. Even the cap on its chimney did not match the others. The resemblance of its ornament to that of the Borden Block and the Rothschild Store, which Sullivan detailed for

---

[70] Irving K Pond, F.A I.A., "Louis Sullivan's 'The Autobiography of an Idea'," *Western Architect*, June 1924, p.68.

[71] *The Economist*, June 24, 1916, July 1, 1916, as quoted in Robert Twombley, *Louis Sullivan, The Public Papers*, pp. 211-222.

[72] Louis H. Sullivan, *The Autobiography of an Idea*, p. 256.

Adler around the same time, suggests that this was the only part of the project, beyond providing the services of a general contractor, with which he was involved.

Edelmann would seem to be the only likely author of the design, but the only logical way to confirm that is to determine if a sufficient number of its features can be found among Edelmann's other earlier and contemporary works to warrant attributing it to him. It has already been noted that in the Grand Opera House, Edelmann relied for the first time upon a profusion of high relief ornaments as architectural elements. On the exterior of the Borden Residence, large relief ornaments also appear as prominent architectural features in their own right. Just as giant rosettes provided a transition element between the ribbed ceiling of the proscenium of the Grand Opera House and the boxes below, similarly large rosettes, located above almost every second floor window, provided a transition between the building's masonry walls and mansard roofs. As evidence of Edelmann's authorship, several identical small panels in the belt course just below the second floor on the north wall (Pl. 38.a.) are of much greater interest. Each, with its elongated stalks of Dresser-like leaves wrapped around three rosettes can confidently be said to be the clearest example of Edelmann's ornamental style as it was at the beginning of 1880. This is an abstract representation of three blossoms of the American Lotus (*Nelumbo lutea*, "the Lotus of the Calumet," which Edelmann was sketching for Irving Pond) surrounded by their entwined stems and leaves.[73] Rosettes: that is, straight on views of blossoms, had long been a favorite Edelmann motif. Stalks of leaves wrapped around them never appear in Sullivan's ornament, but Edelmann would use the same combination of motifs on a slightly larger scale on three occasions shortly thereafter. What is most interesting about these panels, however, is the triangular root at the base from which the lotus springs. This unique feature, never found in Sullivan's ornament, would appear again in almost identical fashion in panels of ornament on the next three buildings on which Edelmann detailed the ornament.

It is the Borden Residence's massive monumentality, which was a basic characteristic of Edelmann's architecture that further establishes it as his work. This was achieved by placing the windows in groups separated by narrow stone piers, by recessing the ornament so that the smooth brick and stone walls would appear as massive as possible and by the use of a heavy battered

---

[73]   Detailed sketches of this plant made by Sullivan in the *Lotos Club Notebook* on August 5, 1875 confirm that this was the source of the detail, see Paul E. Sprague: *The Drawings of Louis Henry Sullivan*, Fig.12.

base to anchor the building to the ground. All these features can be found in Edelmann's work going back to the early 1870s. It would be ten years before Sullivan would achieve a similar monumentality in his own work, when he used the same devices in his preliminary design for the K. A. M. Temple.[74]

---

[74]   Hugh Morrison: *Louis Sullivan, Prophet of Modern Architecture*, 1998 edition, Pl. 43.

CHAPTER 3 - INDEPENDENT PRACTICE IN 1880

By May 1880, Edelmann was listed in the Chicago directory as an architect working on his own and living in the suburb of Oak Park. The 1880 Census entry, taken on June 3rd, also describes him as an architect but states that he and his mother were actually living just to the west of Oak Park in Harlem, Illinois (now called Forest Park).

According to Irving Pond, "Edelmann worked for various architects and iron mongers,"[75] when he opened his own architectural practice, after leaving Dankmar Adler's employ in the spring of 1880. It is unlikely that any documentary evidence will ever be found to credit him with anything he may have done from then until he returned to Cleveland around the end of the year. However, the ornament on two Chicago buildings from this period (the Leopold Strauss Residence, Pls. 11.a. & b., and a factory and showroom building for the C. P. Kimball Carriage Co., Pls. 12a. & b.) was so similar to that of the Grand Opera House, the Borden Residence and the buildings Edelmann designed in 1881 and 1882 in Cleveland, that there can be no doubt that they were substantially Edelmann's work.

The Strauss Residence was an extensive remodeling of the southernmost of three older row houses. (This explains why the property records refer only to the land, not the building, and no building report has ever been found for it.) It also explains why the facade had a Joliet limestone facing, a mansarded top floor and a massive bracketed cornice, all features found on the other two houses. Construction seems to have begun in the summer of 1880, because Water Department records show that a water service was installed there in September,[76] and it was completed in the following year, when the local social register first shows Strauss living there.

Edelmann's desire to maintain a sense of strength and masculinity in his architecture has already been noted. Unlike the Borden Residence, where exploiting its size alone would guarantee the effect of massive strength, this building was relatively small, and its tall and narrow facade had to blend with the restrained Italianate one to which it was attached. There was no room for even a battered base. It is possible that Edelmann found the solution to this problem in Christopher Dresser's *Principles of Decorative Design*. In explaining an illustration (Pl. 40.a.) for an ornament quite similar to that on this building Dresser said,[77]

---

[75]   Letter from Irving K. Pond to Hugh Morrison, April 31, 1932.

[76]   Information provided by Timothy J. Samuelson.

[77]   Christopher Dresser: *Principles of Decorative Design*, 2nd Edition, 1873, pp. 17-18.

". . . I have sought to embody chiefly the idea of power, energy, force, or vigour; and in order to [do] this, I have employed such lines as we see in the bursting buds of spring, when the energy of growth is at its maximum, and especially such as are to be seen in the spring growth of luxuriant tropical vegetation; I have also availed myself of these forms to be seen in certain bones of birds which are associated with the organs of flight, and which give us an impression of great strength, as well as those observable in the powerful propelling fins of certain fish."

Apparently following Dresser's rationale, Edelmann tried to do with ornament what he could not do with mass. For the first time, his stylized foliage grows out in a normal manner only to be bent over upon itself, just like the leaves in Dresser's illustration. This is most obvious in the ornament of the first floor piers (Pl. 40.b.) where the complete lotus motif as it appeared on the panels of the Borden Residence is repeated again.

Other ornamental details on this building can also be found in Edelmann's other work. The stubby spear shaped leaf that first appeared at the outer edge of Edelmann's ornament on the door casings of the St. James Church reappeared here in the capitals of the piers on the facade and again on the interior door casings and the similar caps of the intermediate newel posts of the main stair. The band of projecting squares with small incised rosettes immediately above the boxes in the Grand Opera House reappeared here at the center of the spandrels below all the second floor windows. However, the most important detail tying this building to Edelmann's other work is the root detail at the base of the first floor piers, which is absolutely identical to that on the Borden Residence panels.

While this ornament is similar to Sullivan's at the time, none of it is as lush as his. The edges of the leaves are softer and a blank background, not found in Sullivan's ornament, is common. Hugh Morrison noted the former characteristic when describing the ornament attributed by Pond to Edelmann in the Pullman Building.[78] These differences may also be due to Sullivan's reliance on professional modelers to sculpt whatever ornamental designs he had committed to paper, whereas Edelmann, a skilled sculptor, seems to have supplemented his architectural fees by modeling much of his own ornament. As rapid as Sullivan noted Edelmann was, he still would need to keep this ornament as simple as possible if he were also to have enough time to fulfill his other responsibilities as project architect.

---

[78]   Hugh Morrison: *Louis Sullivan, Prophet of Modern Architecture*, 1998 edition, p. 37.

Except for Edelmann's use of this unique style of ornament, there was nothing remarkable about the Strauss Residence. It was simply one of thousands of similarly composed row houses then being built throughout Chicago.

In spite of the emergence of technologies which made it possible to produce architectural ornament more quickly and abundantly than ever before, its cost remained the deciding factor in how much ornament both Edelmann and Sullivan were able to use. Although seldom if ever recognized, the cost of ornament has always played a critical role in the history of architecture. The restrained elegance of Nicodemus Tessin, the Younger's Royal Palace in Stockholm, for example, was just as much a function of a dearth of expensive materials and highly skilled artisans as it was of the puritanical aspects of the country's Lutheran ethos. Likewise, in the age of the robber barons, architects like Edelmann and Sullivan spent much of their time trying to meet their client's desire for ostentation while at same time spending as little of their money on ornament as possible. Just as Tessin and other Baroque architects had painted plaster or wood to look like marble, Edelmann and Sullivan on occasion tried to make some materials look like other more expensive ones.

The cheapest way to produce elaborate effects is with materials that can be extruded, sawn or turned such as moldings, fretwork and spindles. Anything more elaborate requires the intermediate services of a well-paid modeler to sculpt a pattern from which the finished ornament can be copied in more substantial materials. By the nineteenth century, machinery had been developed which would enable stone and wood ornaments to be carved directly from patterns, but lengthy production time and wear on the cutting surfaces still made sculpted ornaments in those materials the most expensive and therefore generally the least desirable. Once a pattern had been made, however, the technologies of casting iron, stamping sheet metal, firing terra-cotta and molding plaster made it possible to produce a multitude of cheaper copies of a single ornament in those materials. The more copies that could be produced, the cheaper such ornaments would become. Efforts at economy might be further concealed through a mix of such cheaply crafted details mixed with more expensive ones. Edelmann and Sullivan would rely on all these methods, but because Sullivan did not have Edelmann's skills as a sculptor, he was more sensitive to the cost of modeling ornament when it came time to produce it for himself. In the house Sullivan and his brother built for their mother, for example, he was able to avoid hiring a modeler for the elaborate limestone lunette over its entrance by reusing a pattern already made for the Columbian Exposition's Transportation Building.

Circumstantial evidence also exists to connect Edelmann to the Kimball Building. On September 19, 1880, it was announced that the plans were in preparation, the ground had been broken and the owner, David W. Irwin, had commissioned his architect, Cyrus P. Thomas (one of a prominent family of Canadian architects, who had come to Chicago in 1870) to build a five story building to be leased to the Kimball company.[79] Since 1876, Charles P. Kimball had been planning to move his family and business from New York to Chicago. At that time, he was already in negotiations with Irwin about building a factory nearby.[80] It seems more than a coincidence that, while Edelmann was still in Cleveland in 1882, Kimball fulfilled his ambitions by hiring Edelmann's Chicago associates, Dankmar Adler and his junior partner Louis Sullivan, to design a large residence for him and his family in Chicago.

One final connection is suggested by Irving Pond's remark that Edelmann was also employed by, "various . . . iron-mongers." No maker's marks were ever found on its cast iron, but the Kimball Building along with all the designs for its ground floor pilasters and interior columns (Pl. 39.), several variations on the same themes and a detail Sullivan himself later used were illustrated in the Union Foundry's *Manual Illustrating a Few Patterns for Architectural Iron Work* in 1886.[81] Perhaps it was someone at the Union Foundry who provided Edelmann with an introduction to either Thomas or Kimball.

The facades of the Kimball Building seem to have been the work of both Thomas and Edelmann. The slightly projecting bays, topped by pyramidal and mansarded roofs were all standard devices used by Thomas on other work at that time.[82] Masonry facades supported at the ground floor on exposed cast iron store fronts had been a familiar feature of Thomas's work ever since he first used them in a number of buildings on Granville Street in Halifax, Nova Scotia in 1860.[83] There his influence on the design seems to have ended. Neither his preferences for dividing facades horizontally at each floor by a continuous projecting sill course nor the use of the identical fenestration at

---

[79]   *Chicago Tribune*, September 19, 1880.

[80]   *Chicago Tribune*, September 3, 1876.

[81]   A copy is in the Chicago Historical Society Library. The Union Foundry was established prior to 1880, but did not establish its relationship with Pullman until somewhat later. The tie rod caps which Sullivan used on the residence that Adler & Sullivan designed for Eli. B. Felsenthal in 1885 are identical to the large rosettes on the cast iron piers of the ground floor of the Kimball Building. They too appeared in the Union Foundry catalog.

[82]   The still extant Farewell House, northeast corner of Jackson Blvd. & Halsted Street and Delaware Building, northeast corner of Dearborn and Randolph Streets and the no longer extant Richelieu Hotel, all in Chicago.

[83]   Glen McArthur and Annie Szamosi: *William Thomas, Architect, 1799-1860*, p. 134.

each floor (which went all the way back to his days in Canada) were evident here. Beginning with the Moody Tabernacle and ending with the ten story Decker Building in New York, Edelmann had a preference for tying the windows of his multistory buildings together into no more than two story increments (referred to hereafter as "vertically paired fenestration"). Here that preference, in opposition to Thomas's, was evident at the third and fourth floors.

Whatever compromises Edelmann may have had to make with Thomas, all of the ornamental details were undoubtedly his. The terra-cotta spandrels (Pl. 38.b.) again featured lotus blossom-like rosettes similar to those found on the Borden Residence panel. These particular rosettes are one of the clearest examples of Edelmann's occasional tendency to portray plant forms in a natural rather than abstracted manner. With the rare exception of the use of a corn cob motif, this was one Edelmann practice that Sullivan avoided. The leaves, however, were no longer clearly those of the lotus. They had become more abstract and were again bent back upon themselves like those on the Strauss Residence. These large fluted leaves would remain a prominent feature of Edelmann's later work. Perched on the edge of their stalks as they passed over the top of each rosette was what looked vaguely like a pair of fish hooks. Comparison with a prominent Edelmann ornament in the light court of the Blackstone—Perkins Power Building built a year later (Pl. 41.b.) reveals that these were really squashed versions of his typical spear shaped leaf. The large turned roundels between each of the brackets in the roof cornice were also related to those above the three first floor windows at the east end of the south wall of the Borden Residence (Pl. 10.).

The capitals of the cast iron pilasters of the ground floor (Pl. 39.) were similar to their counterparts on the front of the Strauss Residence. The central motif on their bases had already appeared on the pilasters of the lower level boxes of the Grand Opera House and in a simplified version at the top of the piers of the living room of the Strauss Residence. Here again was a stylized representation of the lotus complete with stem, leaves and root.

With the exception of a single stone ornament on the Harrison Street front, all of the ornament was manufactured in quantity from a total of only five different patterns, two of which were mere belt courses. The simplicity of all these pieces again suggests that Edelmann modeled them.

In early promotional woodcuts of the building (Pl. 12.b.), each side of the mansarded roof of the main corner tower features a very prominent dormer. These do not appear in any of the known photographs of the building (all taken after the tower was rebuilt following a fire in 1897). The remarkable resemblance of the tower in these woodcuts to the top of the tower on the Central School in New Philadelphia, Ohio, for which Edelmann appears to have been the construction superintendent, suggests that its treatment may have been inspired by the memory of that Alexander Koehler design.

CHAPTER 4 - RETURN TO CLEVELAND 1881-1883

Sometime after November 17, 1880 when Sullivan drew a portrait of him, Edelmann gave up his Chicago practice and again returned to Cleveland. Exactly what prompted this move is not known, but the circumstances surrounding it suggest some possible reasons. Upon their return to Cleveland, his mother went to live with the Bluims, her eldest daughter's family, while he took up residence nearby. This suggests that family considerations may have played a role. That Edelmann was almost immediately employed by architects Coburn & Barnum to take charge of two building projects for developer Jacob B. Perkins might also suggest that through his Cleveland connections he had received a job offer from them that was substantial enough to justify terminating his Chicago practice.

Of the eleven Coburn & Barnum buildings known to have been designed in 1881, all were residences, except the two commercial buildings that Edelmann built for them.[84] His substantial experience in both the design and construction of commercial buildings in Chicago would at that point have been invaluable to them. The working drawings for the first of these, the Climax Building, had already been completed. Edelmann appears to have only superintended its construction. It is likely that the preliminary designs for the second project, an office and manufacturing building collectively referred to here as the Blackstone—Perkins Power Building, had already been worked out by Forrest Coburn, the senior partner of the firm. Edelmann was nevertheless given the responsibility of not only constructing it but also of preparing the working drawings and defining its ornamental treatment.

Although the two halves of the Blackstone—Perkins Power Building served different functions, architecturally and structurally it was a single five story building with a fully mansarded top floor. The division between the two halves was marked roughly near the center of its longest facade by a six story tower, the base of which contained the main entrance to the Perkins Power part of the building, a loft structure intended primarily for manufacturing and supplied with a large steam power plant for the use of the tenants. The Blackstone half was built primarily to provide office space for lawyers, hence its being named after the famous English jurist.

At least one contemporary source cites Edelmann as one of the building's designers and superintendent of its construction while working for Coburn

---

[84] List of buildings of the firm and short biography of Forrest Amos Coburn provided by Robert Keiser of the Cleveland Landmarks Commission.

and Barnum.[85] Years later, Perkins himself would note that the architect of the Wilshire Building (which was definitely Edelmann's work) was also the architect of this building.[86] Nevertheless, Edelmann's role as a designer on this project appears to have been limited primarily if not exclusively to its ornament. Ornamental details in his unique style which appear in the surviving construction drawings (Pl. 13) also indicate that they were prepared under his direction.

In the Kimball Building, Edelmann's architectural expression was limited by the work of the other project architect, C. P. Thomas. In the Blackstone—Perkins Power Building, he appears to have worked in an even more restricted role for architects Coburn and Barnum. The overall massing of this building has much in common with the Borden Residence, which may have helped Edelmann in making their basic design somewhat his own. The real source of the design, however, is clearly the work of Richard Morris Hunt, for whom Forrest Coburn, the senior partner of the firm, had worked prior to 1877.[87] The similarity of the main front of the Blackstone part of the building to Hunt's Delaware and Hudson Canal Company Building in New York of 1876 is obvious. The similarity of the tower of the adjoining Perkins Power section with that of Hunt's Tribune Building in New York of the same year is only slightly less so.[88] Given their dates, Coburn might even have worked on these buildings. It seems unlikely that Coburn, as a protege of Hunt (then one of America's most prominent architects) would have allowed Edelmann to alter his design significantly. That this was the case is evident not only in the minimal resemblance it has to Edelmann's own previous work, but in the use of consoles springing from the piers below to support the main roof cornice. This detail, never used elsewhere by Edelmann, would appear again in Coburn and Barnum's Furniture Block a year after he left their employ[89] and had also appeared in a preliminary design for Hunt's Delaware and Hudson Canal Company Building.[90]

Sculpted ornament on the exterior was rather sparse except for the elaborate dormer panels (where the root detail of the Borden Residence panel appeared again) a narrow row of leaves at the top of each of the first floor piers and the carved lintels over the two main entrances. According to family tradition, the

---

[85] *Penny Press* (Cleveland), May 29, 1882.

[86] Note, inside its front cover, identifying the authorship of the child's alphabet book made for Perkins' son. Preserved in the Western Reserve Historical Society as MS. 3227.

[87] Obituary in *Cleveland Press,* December 2, 1897. Clipping provided by Robert Keiser.

[88] See photographs of these in Paul R. Baker: *Richard Morris Hunt,* Fig. 42 & Fig. 43.

[89] Eric Johannesen, *Cleveland Architecture 1876 -1976,* p.10.

[90] Susan R. Stein: *The Architecture of Richard Morris Hunt,* fig. 3.

bust of Blackstone over the Blackstone entrance (Pl. 41.a.) and the arm and hammer over the Perkins Power entrance were sculpted by Edelmann. Like the Borden Residence panels and the spandrels of the Kimball Building, each of the two ornaments framing the bust featured a prominent rosette entwined in foliage. Even though the petals of these rosettes are treated in the same natural fashion as those in the Kimball Building spandrels, the source here does not seem to have been "the Lotus of the Calumet" which suggests that perhaps Edelmann was seeking inspiration for his plant forms locally.

In the interior light court of the Blackstone, there were several ornamental details that had already appeared on both the Strauss Residence and the Kimball Building. The large spandrel panels on the walls (Pl. 41.b.) were the most notable. Each of these identical panels featured all the sculpted motifs already seen in those buildings: fluted, fish hook, spear and bent leaves, rosettes and the same new spiral fluted leaf on the lintel over the building's entrance. Looking at these panels, there can be no doubt that the ornaments on all three buildings were done by the same hand. The large surface of blank background again suggests that Edelmann modeled these panels himself. In addition to this ornament, the two different types of the newel post caps had already appeared in the interior trim of the Strauss Residence. A later section of the building in the collections of the Western Reserve Historical Society shows that even the balustrades of the stairs were originally made up of turned balusters similar to those on the stairs of the Strauss Residence.[91]

According to family tradition, while with Coburn and Barnum, Edelmann also designed the catafalque for President James Garfield's body when it lay in state in Cleveland's Public Square in September 1881.[92] The design of the baldachin which sheltered the coffin itself seems to be the only part of this project which can with any confidence be attributed to Edelmann. It consisted of a simply draped cloth supported at each corner by a massive, gilded mast with an Edelmann-like base.[93] Above and completely surrounding this was a massive four arched canopy, reminiscent of both a canopy designed by Hunt in 1868 for the tomb of Robert Fulton and the Meadowport Arch designed by Calvert Vaux for Prospect Park in Brooklyn in the same year.[94] Since Coburn

---

[91]   The wire lattices seen in surviving photographs were apparently later alterations.

[92]   "In Search of John Edelmann," *A.I.A. Journal*, February 1966, p. 37.

[93]   The same concave cone shaped base detail had already appeared in the dormers of the Borden Residence and the columns at the opening between the front and rear parlors of the Strauss Residence and would later appear in the top floor of the Gilman Building.

[94]   Francis R. Kowsky: *Country, Park & City, The Architecture and Life of Calvert Vaux,* Fig. 7.3; Susan R. Stein: *The Architecture of Richard Morris Hunt,* fig. 7.

could very likely have seen these precedents while working for Hunt, Coburn was likely the author of this part of the project.

Unique among Edelmann's known work is an alphabet book he made for Perkins' young son Guy.[95] The photograph which the prominent Cleveland photographer James F. Ryder took of Edelmann around this time (Frontispiece) confirms that his portrayals under "D" of a "draughtsman" and under "I" of an inspector are actually self-portraits. That he portrayed himself in this way suggests that he made the book while still employed by Coburn & Barnum. That it was done without their knowledge is further suggested by his portrayal of an architect under "A" as an elderly bearded man, which looks nothing like one of the firm's partners but strongly resembles C. P. Thomas.

The craftsmanship which he put into this child's book was of the highest order and must have required considerable time and a well-equipped workshop to complete. The perfection with which the identical carved walnut front and back covers (Pl. 42.a.) are executed should dispel any question as to his abilities as a sculptor. The spine is of heavy, very durable leather. A brass clasp originally held the covers together, but the locking bar attached to the back cover has been ripped off. This is the only damage the book has suffered since it was made. Each page is of a thick lightly enameled paper attached to the binding by a heavy blue cloth hinge.

Edelmann's characteristic ornaments appear both on the covers and every page of the book. In each lower corner of the covers is a more fully developed form of the V-shaped motif that had first been suggested in his work on the St. James Church and Sinai Temple seven years before. In each upper corner, four fluted leaves spring from a central point. Between these, natural looking narrow petaled blossoms repeat continuously along the outer edges. These appear to be a slightly abstracted version of a mustard blossom.[96] All of these motifs would find their way into some of the buildings both Edelmann and Sullivan designed in the coming years. On the last page, which Edelmann somewhat humorously allotted, "For the man who could not be found," he entwined the letter "Z" (Pl. 42.b.) with an elaborate garland that is reminiscent of the hinges on the doors of the St. James Church.

Whether the book was made as a gift to the son of a man Edelmann had developed great affection for or was made to secure Perkins' patronage, we will never know, but if it was for the latter, it succeeded. By February 1882,

---

[95]   Preserved in the Western Reserve Historical Society as MS. 3227.

[96]   This motif would also appear about the same time in a terra-cotta spandrel presumably designed by Sullivan for Dankmar Adler's Rosenfeld Building. See Fig. 7 in *Louis H. Sullivan Architectural Ornament Collection, Southern Illinois University at Edwardsville.*

Perkins had ended his relationship with Coburn & Barnum and turned over three of his other projects, the Wilshire, the Stephens & Widlar and the Gilman buildings to Edelmann.[97] These become critical in the analysis of Edelmann's work because they are the only buildings for which he is actually credited as sole architect before he left the Midwest in 1887. The Wilshire Building was a six story office building begun early in 1882.[98] The Stephens & Widlar Building begun in the summer of 1882[99] was a five story loft building to be used primarily for manufacturing. The still extant Gilman Building is a five story store and office building begun late in 1882.[100]

In the months after Edelmann left his office, Dankmar Adler received the commissions to design the six story Borden Block (no longer extant, northwest corner of Randolph and Dearborn streets, Chicago) and a five story store building for E. Rothschild & Brothers (no longer extant, 212 W. Monroe Street, Chicago, Pl. 29.) both of which would have an obvious impact on Edelmann's approach to the design of all three of these buildings. In the Borden Block, for the first time in Adler's work, the masonry piers which carried the wall and floor loads down to the building's isolated spread footings became the most noticeable feature of the facades. At the first two floors these piers were separated from each other by the same kind of cast iron framed store fronts Adler had just used in the Central Music Hall. In the Rothschild Store, this approach was carried to its next logical step by extending the cast iron elements through the full height of the building, producing a facade dominated by glass and iron.

The site of the Wilshire Building (Pl. 14.) was not very conducive to the construction of an efficient office building. Because it was sandwiched between two other buildings, windows could only be put in its relatively narrow front and rear walls. To provide adequate natural light throughout the building, Edelmann arranged all of its six floors around a glass roofed interior light court, defined at the sides by square cast iron columns on the ground floor and round cast iron, vaguely Ionic columns with elaborate cast iron guard rails at each of the upper floors. In obedience to Eidlitz's concept of an organic architecture, the presence of this light court was reflected on the facade by placing its two central stone pilasters in line with the internal rows of columns which defined it. Although the column at the center of the first two floors carried as much weight as the pilasters, it was significantly

---

[97] Drawings in the collections of the Western Reserve Historical Society show that in later years, when Edelmann was no longer in Cleveland, he again retained Coburn and Barnum for other commercial work.

[98] *Leader* (Cleveland), February 28, 1882.

[99] *American Architect*, July 15, 1882.

[100] *American Architect*, October 7, 1882.

narrower, expressing not only the nature of the material but also that the space behind the first internal bay was essentially empty. As impressive as this court must have been, by the end of the century the skylight had been removed, the cast iron columns bricked over and the spaces between them glazed to form a rather ordinary exterior light court.[101]

Now that Edelmann was again on his own, he returned to the approach which he and Adler had developed for the State Street front of the Central Music Hall for the front of the Wilshire Building. Thus, the first two floors of both buildings were faced with expansive glass display windows framed in ornate cast iron between narrow stone piers which supported the stone walls of the office floors above. The repetition of arched and flat headed windows in every other floor of the Central Music Hall had not only met Edelmann's preference for vertically paired fenestration but gave the facade some clarity. Such restrained detailing would, however, no longer suffice to meet the taste for lavish ornament, which Edelmann had come to indulge in.

The Wilshire Building was undoubtedly one of the most ornate designs Edelmann produced. In spite of its truthful expression of structure and function, it was, nevertheless, also his least coherent. This seems to have evolved from the way the project began. An early description of the building says that it would be, "surmounted by a high French roof and a handsome tower," like those on the Blackstone Building.[102] In the executed design these features were replaced by an elaborate extension of the front wall (Pl. 43.a.) which Edelmann obviously found the inspiration for in the ornate top floor of Adler's Rothschild Store. This change may simply have been a whim on Edelmann's part, but since the size and number of the windows in it were the same as in the floors below, it seems more likely that it was an effort, possibly suggested by his client, to make the top floor more desirable for office space than it would have been if faced with the dormers of a mansard roof.

Heavily rusticated floors were often effectively used at grade level to visually tie a facade to the ground or to provide a transition at the top between a mansard roof and the floors below. By inserting one at the third floor level in roughly the middle of the facade, this feature not only needlessly accentuated

---

[101] The appearance of this light court is documented in a halftone longitudinal section of the building. It, together with two loose floor plans in the collections of the Western Reserve Historical Society, probably came from a rental brochure. The elaborate detailing of the section suggests that it was drawn by Edelmann. The reworking of the light court is documented in drawings by Coburn and Barnum also at the Western Reserve Historical Society. A fire originating in the Perkins-Power Building in 1897 resulted in the destruction of its tower roof. The damage caused by the spread of this fire to the Wilshire may have been the reason for reworking the light court.

[102] *Leader* (Cleveland) February 28, 1882.

the differences between the stores of the first two floors and the offices above, but left the distinctly incongruous impression of one building standing upon another. Edelmann seems to have been too competent an architect to have deliberately chosen to do this. More likely he was stuck with stonework already fabricated for the mansarded solution and had little choice other than to compose the facade in the way it was built.

Somewhat suggestive of the Art Nouveau is an unexecuted project for an entrance to the upper floors of the building. This project, which is documented in a skillfully executed water color perspective signed, "J. H. Edelma[nn], Archit[ect]," at the Western Reserve Historical Society (Pl. 15.), called for a half domed canopy supported by curved cast iron brackets and topped by a crest of leaf ornament.[103]

Edelmann's appreciation for Adler's achievement in the Rothschild Store becomes fully evident in his design for the Stephens & Widlar Building (Pl. 16.). The one feature which detracted from the structural logic of Adler's building was Sullivan's riot of ornament and arches decorating its top floor. A more logical expression would have been evident to Edelmann in the Leiter Building built the year before immediately to the east, across the alley from the Rothschild Store, but there W. L. B. Jenney, its architect, had compromised the expression of the cast iron facade system by bricking in the spandrels and capping the entire building with a brick cornice. In the Stephens & Widlar Building, Edelmann attempted to resolve these inconsistencies by adopting Adler's use of a cast iron framed curtain wall between masonry piers and arranging all its members on a rectilinear grid. Although his solution was better than Adler's, it was not entirely successful. Here again the round banded cast iron columns of the store front facade at the first two floors were similar to those first used on the Central Music Hall and subsequently on the Borden Block and the Wilshire Building. For no structural or functional reason, Edelmann doubled the cast iron mullions in the top floor. Apparently he could not get beyond his preference for vertically paired fenestration.

Having just exploited the possibilities of a cast iron front, Edelmann's treatment of the facades (now covered over with a metal skin) of the Gilman Building (Pl. 17.) is disappointing. Here the walls are entirely of masonry construction, with the exception of the iron lintels above the first floor openings. The arrangement of the fenestration with large floor to ceiling display windows on the first two floors and much narrower windows in

---

[103] The edges of this perspective have been trimmed down with a scissors cutting off the last letters of the credit line and most likely the kind of ornamental border that Edelmann typically placed on his presentation drawings.

the upper three floors suggests that the former were originally intended for mercantile use while the latter were intended for office or manufacturing use. It may have been this program which suggested Adler's Borden Block as a prototype. Whatever the source of the design, it resembles the Borden Block more than any other work of either Edelmann, Adler or Sullivan. The narrow width of the building seems to have determined that the bay at the corner and those on the St. Clair Street side would have to be relatively narrow like those of the Borden Block. Another feature found on the Borden Block is the use of stone columns between the windows on the top floor (each with a basket capital similar to those first seen in the St. James Church seven years before). Even though these windows were of the same width as those below, this subtle change meant that, in deference to Edelmann's preference for vertically paired fenestration, they were treated differently from those of the two floors beneath them. Although the fenestration of the first two floors was almost as generous as that of the Wilshire and Stephens & Widlar buildings, it is capped at the second floor of each bay by a heavy arch. These arches provide, however, a far more effective transition between the two story storefronts and the floors above than the rusticated third floor of the Wilshire Building. As on the Wilshire and Stephens & Widlar buildings, prominent projecting piers ran the full height of the building. Edelmann's preference for a transitional element between ground and wall had not been effectively realized in any of his earlier Cleveland buildings. In each case all he could do without narrowing the store front windows was to widen the piers outward at the base. That does not seem to have been a consideration here. Free to widen the piers to the sides as well, he designed massive stone plinths which visually anchor the piers to the ground, in the same way that the battered bases of the piers had on the front of the Sinai Temple.

The most elaborate ornament on the building is the long narrow spandrel panel above the first floor corner entrance (now covered over, Pl. 43.b.). This ornament features the same leaf forms which first appeared in the Strauss Residence and Kimball Building three years earlier, and it also features a clearer version of the mustard blossom on the covers of the Guy Perkins alphabet book. In spite of these similarities to Edelmann's earlier work, the ornament on this building is different. All the discordant elements that first appeared in the ornament of the Strauss Residence had disappeared. This ornament bears a distinct resemblance to Sullivan's at the time, as if to suggest that Edelmann was readying himself to return to Chicago to work with Adler & Sullivan. That the elaborate metal brackets on the piers at the second floor had already been strongly hinted at a year earlier in the top of Sullivan's design of the central piers of the Academy of Music in Kalamazoo (Pl. 31.)

39

would seem to suggest a Sullivan influence. Nevertheless the detail at the base of these brackets, when turned to face upward, (Pl. 44.a.) has a distinct resemblance to the caps of the newel posts of the parapet of the organ loft of the St. James Church and would soon appear again in the work of Adler & Sullivan while Edelmann was working for them. Thus used, it might best be referred to as his "fanned lotus".

On November 14, 1882 during construction of the Gilman Building, a derrick designed by Edelmann and used previously by him on the Wilshire Building collapsed, killing four men.[104] Although some questions were raised in the press as to who was at fault, Edelmann was never formally blamed for the collapse, and in the end he appears to have suffered no loss from it.

Edelmann was last listed as living in Cleveland in the directory published in July 1883, shortly after the Gilman Building had been completed.

---

[104] Edelmann may be seen standing behind two men looking at the construction drawings in a photograph of this scaffold when in use on the Wilshire Building. This is reproduced at full size in Eric Johannesen: *Cleveland Architecture 1876-1976*, p. 6.

CHAPTER 5 - COMEDOWN, RETURN TO CHICAGO
1883-1887

Most likely because of a job offer from the newly formed firm of Adler & Sullivan, Architects, Edelmann returned to Chicago (this time without his mother) in the summer of 1883 to become its foreman. A perspective for a double house, dated 1883 (Pl. 18.) and Edelmann's hand written instructions at the bottom of a drawing for new glass in the doors of Adler & Sullivan's office in the Borden Block irrefutably confirm Edelmann's employment by the firm.[105] The pen and ink drawing of the double house not only bears the firm's credit line written in his distinctive hand, but also features a typical Edelmann border of the type found on his two published drawings of 1874 and on each page of the Guy Perkins alphabet book as well as various drafting techniques unique to him.

Three other perspectives bear similar handwritten credit lines, but only one of them, a drawing of the Troescher Building published in the Inland Architect in December 1884 (Pl. 35.), appears to have been entirely Edelmann's work. The other two, both published in 1885, appear to have been begun by him but completed by two different draftsmen, which helps to confirm that Edelmann was by then no longer working for the firm.[106]

Edelmann's services would certainly have been needed because in the year and a half he would work for Adler & Sullivan, the firm would have about forty commissions, roughly twice as much work as it had during the same previous and succeeding period. This sudden prosperity would certainly have put both Adler and Sullivan in a bind, but they each knew from experience that they could rely on Edelmann to help pull them out of it. With no sign of new work coming in the near future in Cleveland, Edelmann would have had little choice but to put himself again under the oversight of Adler and the man he had put forward only three years earlier to replace him as Adler's assistant. Having just designed and built three substantial commercial buildings on his

---

[105] Edelmann's distinctive handwriting may be seen in the *Lotos Club Notebook* and his letters in the Western Reserve Historical Society collections. Among its numerous peculiarities, the most noticeable are stringing words together without a break and the use, often within the same document, of two forms of lower case "e": the standard single loop and a two looped miniaturized upper case version of that letter. For the office door detail see Robert Twombley & Narciso G. Menocal: *Louis Sullivan, The Poetry of Architecture*, Drawing 88.

[106] A perspective completed by Henry Schlacks of the Ryerson Building in *Inland Architect* of May 1885 and a perspective completed by Paul Lautrup of the McVickers Theatre (a project begun in 1883) in *American Architect* of March 14, 1885.

own in Cleveland, this could only have been an irksome comedown. This seems to explain why not long after his return to Chicago in the winter of 1883 to 84, he sought outside work in the office of S. S. Beman designing the iron staircases and elevator grills of the Pullman Building, as Irving Pond testified.[107] Unfortunately none of Edelmann's work on the elevators was documented before the building was demolished in 1957, but a photograph of a run of the iron staircases has recently been found. Although a repeating "9" shaped leaf motif in the scroll at the end of each tread, which Edelmann had previously used in the various segmental pediments at the top of both the Blackstone and Wilshire buildings, confirms Pond's testimony, aside from it and a few other minor Edelmann motifs, these stairways differed in no significant way from those in other Beman buildings of the period. Thus it seems that with less freedom to do things his way than Sullivan was willing to allow him, Edelmann did not pursue further work with Beman.

Edelmann was surely not Adler's only former employee enlisted to help meet the expanded work load. Among the firm's work at this time was a row of three houses for Max M. Rothschild (no longer extant, 3201-05 S. Indiana Avenue, Chicago). Even though Hugh Morrison made something of its simplicity,[108] suggesting that it might even prefigure Sullivan's later work, it did not resemble any project Sullivan is known to have previously produced. In fact the only feature of its design which is even remotely suggested in his work was the configuration of the second floor sash. With its bracketed cornice and smooth Joilet stone front, this essentially Italianate building bore an obvious resemblance to the Crilly & Blair Building (no longer extant, southeast corner of Halsted and Madison streets, Chicago) built by Adler's firm in early 1880 and a three story building credited to C. P. Thomas (no longer extant, southwest corner of Harrison Street and Wabash Avenue, Chicago) across from the Kimball Building, which was completed immediately before construction of the Kimball Building began. Although Edelmann was working for both firms around the time these buildings were erected, none of them had even a passing resemblance to his known work. It seems likely that all three were designed by Edelmann's former partner, Joseph S. Johnston, whose ability to design in the Italianate style has already been noted. Not only was Johnston sharing office space with Adler in 1879 when the Crilly & Blair seems to have been designed, but also from 1880 onward, he was listed in the directories as working on his own, which would have allowed him to easily assist other firms.

---

[107] Letter from Irving K. Pond to Hugh Morrison, April 31, 1932.

[108] Hugh Morrison: *Louis Sullivan, Prophet of Modern Architecture*, 1998 edition, p. 49, Pl. 13.

The double house in Edelmann's perspective seems to have been designed for a Mr. Straus and was intended to cover the full width of three lots at 2441 to 2445 S. Wabash Avenue in Chicago.[109] A building report in Inland Architect for June 1884 suggests, by the cited 42 foot width of the building, that by that date Adler & Sullivan had been forced to reduce its size to fit on only the two northernmost lots. The Robinson insurance map for 1886 confirms that a brick duplex of approximately that width had been erected on this property and that the third lot remained vacant. Unfortunately no illustration of the completed building has been found to confirm that it was Adler & Sullivan's work. This project is unique among the early work of Adler & Sullivan. While the general composition of each of the identical houses is reminiscent of the Ann Halsted Residence (extant, 440 W. Belden Avenue, Chicago) which was undoubtedly designed by Sullivan at the beginning of 1883, their massive simplicity and Tudor character is not even remotely suggested in any of Adler & Sullivan's other residences of the period. Three features unique to this design (elliptically arched, triple first floor windows; the columns between the two outer third floor windows, and the coursed ashlar masonry surrounding the entrances) can all be found in Edelmann's Cleveland work but had never been previously used by Sullivan. This suggests that Edelmann was not only responsible for the perspective but also for the design of the building itself. Absent, however, is any suggestion of a battered base. The absence of even a suggestion of one on every building designed after Sullivan replaced Edelmann as Adler's foreman suggests that Sullivan did not like such bases and had instructed Edelmann not to use them.

Edelmann's influence on the work of Adler & Sullivan from mid-1883 to the beginning of 1885 is clearly evident in the use of certain ornamental details peculiar to his Cleveland work that only appear in the firm's work at that time. The most obvious of these, his fanned lotus, was to appear on at least thirteen of the projects undertaken by the firm beginning with the Knisely Store and Flats (Pl. 19.) and ending with the Opera Festival Hall, begun and completed in the first three months of 1885, which was a temporary remodeling of the interior of the Interstate Industrial Exhibition Building located where the Chicago Art Institute now stands.

A permit for the Knisely Store and Flats was issued in June 1883, before Edelmann returned to Chicago, but by September a reference to plans only

---

[109] This location is confirmed by the shadows on the perspective, the building report and the fact that the insurance map shows only one brick duplex on either side of the 2400 block of Wabash Ave. The insurance map further confirms that the adjoining lots met the conditions shown in the perspective.

having been prepared suggests that its construction had not yet begun.[110] Sullivan may therefore have been responsible for the basic design of the building, but its front can easily be attributed to Edelmann. His fanned lotuses appeared as pinnacles at the roof line and the coursed ashlar pilasters framing its first floor store fronts were almost identical to those on the first two floors of both the Wilshire and Stephens & Widlar buildings. Both of these features also appear on the still extant Kaufmann Store and Flats built at about the same time. The most interesting ornaments on the Knisely Store and Flats were above its central second and third floor windows. The tympanum of the third floor arch featured the repeating "9" shaped leaf motif of the segmental pediments at the top of both the Blackstone and Wilshire buildings. The spandrel above the second floor window, on the other hand, had no precedent in either Edelmann's or Sullivan's work. It is a highly abstracted image of a plant, which with its dangling root nevertheless seems attributable to Edelmann.

The prominent use of Edelmann's fanned lotus as well as the same narrow columns and handrail details found on the double house perspective establish that the Solomon Blumenfeld Flats (Pl. 20.) was also primarily Edelmann's work. Here Edelmann's preference for vertically paired fenestration was again clearly evident.

How the sculpted ornament on the early work of Adler & Sullivan and its immediate predecessors was designed is an aspect of their work that has received no attention. The use of slightly modified versions of certain basic ornaments in these buildings indicates that in order to facilitate rapid production of the drawings of these details, prototype drawings must have been prepared by Sullivan which were then turned over to the firm's draftsmen to modify as they saw fit to meet the requirements of any particular project to which they were assigned. One of the most obvious examples of this is a dominant question mark shaped leaf from which other leaves spring. This usually appears at the top of vertical elements. One of the earliest examples of this was the motif at the top of the piers between the first floor windows of the Hammond Library (Pl. 33.). Since it was designed in 1882, the detail must be Sullivan's, but the way it is treated at either side of the entrance to the Blumenfeld Flats and at the top of the piers at the ends of the Knisely Building's store fronts seems to reveal something about how Edelmann and Sullivan responded to each other in their now reversed roles. Both seem to be deliberate parodies on Edelmann's part of this rather squat prototype. In the Blumenfeld detail, Edelmann translated it into an elegant, almost sublime,

---

[110]   *American Architect*, June 16, 1883, September 15, 1883.

form. In the Knisely Building, the effect was reversed. The detail was blown out of proportion into a gargantuan feature. Perhaps Edelmann was trying to show Sullivan who was still the master, but Sullivan was apparently not ready to take the hint. Although Edelmann would devise another version of this detail once he was again on his own, neither of his revised versions of it would ever again appear in Adler & Sullivan's work.

The other nine Adler & Sullivan buildings from this same period where Edelmann's fanned lotuses appear are the following (the number in italics refers to their position in the list of Sullivan's work in the 1998 revised edition of Hugh Morrison's *Louis Sullivan, Prophet of Modern Architecture*):

1 (*37*). Morris Selz Residence.
2 (*46*). Louis E. Frank Residence.
3 (*47*). Martin Barbe Residence.
4 (*51*). F. A. Kennedy & Co. Bakery.
5 (*54*). Anna McCormick Residence.
6 (*59*). Ryerson Building.
7 (*60*). Leon Mannheimer Residence.
8 (*61*). Troescher Building.
9 (*64*). Ruben Rubel Residence.

In spite of the use of this fanned lotus motif and related ornaments of the same style, there is only a minimal amount of similarity between these buildings. Here, as in the Rothschild Rowhouses, this was apparently due to the projects having been designed either in whole or in part by different individuals.

By the end of the century, a fixed division of labor had become characteristic of the largest architectural offices, but as is still the case today, the responsibilities of each employee in a small office like Adler & Sullivan might vary from day to day depending on what was needed at the moment to meet the workload. The still common belief that the principals of any firm must be the people solely responsible for the esthetic of a firm's output has seldom been true.

Although the three commercial buildings cited above featured ornamental motifs which could have been designed by Edelmann, Sullivan or both, the preferences each man had for arranging either façade bays or fenestration is not evident in any of them. This suggests that Adler was entirely in control of their structural design. The Kennedy Bakery (no longer extant, 27-37 N. Desplaines St., Chicago) was the least ornate of the three. Its greatly simplified versions of Edelmann's fanned lotuses suggests that his design role was minimal, if he was involved with it at all. In the Troescher Building (no longer extant, 15-19 S. Wacker Dr., Chicago, Pl. 35.) and the Ryerson Building (no longer extant, 16-20 E. Randolph St. Chicago) the system of main supporting masonry piers Adler first employed in the Rothschild Store was used again but instead of supporting the spandrels on intervening cast iron columns, their weight was distributed back to the piers on iron lintels. The elaborate decorative devices (the arched ground floor and humped cornice of the Troescher Building and the bulging bays of the Ryerson Building) which either Edelmann, Sullivan or both contributed, only compromised the expression of their otherwise rather bold structural systems. These buildings, therefore, appear to have been the work of a team of designers rather than one person.

That also appears to have been the case with the residential buildings, but in the Frank, McCormick and Barbe residences, Edelmann's influence seems to have been more pronounced than in the others. Not only were these the only houses erected by the firm up to that time to feature wood verandas, but the verandas themselves feature spindled shed roof gables unique to Edelmann's later work. Sandwiched between party walls with their two story bays and third floor mansards, the general conception of the Frank and McCormick residences was essentially the same.

With its smooth brownstone facing, the Louis E. Frank Residence (Pl. 21.) was similar in form if not in color to Edelmann's Strauss Residence. The tower capped dormer at the top of the Strauss Residence's bay was here replaced by an equally prominent stone dormer topped by a sheet metal pediment featuring one of Edelmann's fanned lotuses set against a sunburst background. The simplicity of this brownstone front and the treatment of the squared basket capitals in the dormer indicates that by this time, Edelmann was becoming aware of Richardson's work. This is confirmed by the use of similar columns in his Richardson inspired design for the Eighth Avenue front of The Gospel Tabernacle (Pl. 26.) in New York four years later.

In spite of the position of many of its horizontal elements having been determined by those of the adjoining monochromatic Selz Residence, the front of the Anna McCormick Residence (Pl. 22.) was of an entirely different character. The natural colors of its light stone base, the red brick and terra-cotta of its masonry walls and the slate mansard are clearly evident. Even the wood veranda and sheet metal trim may have been painted in contrasting colors. To further enliven the design the projecting bay was two sided with a prominent pilaster topped by one of Edelmann's fanned lotuses accenting the point where its planes met. Here Edelmann's preference for vertically paired fenestration is as clearly evident as it was in the Blumenfeld Flats. An expansive triple window in the third floor mansard of the type first used by Edelmann on the

Gilman Building and later by him on his double house design provided an even more forceful accent to the top of the bay than the stone dormer had on the Frank Residence. The prominent piers framing this window were in turn topped by even larger fanned lotus pinacles reminiscent of the fanned lotus pinacles on the Blumenfeld Flats.

The Martin Barbe Residence (Pl. 23) was unique among Adler & Sullivan's early houses. While the others conformed to row house prototypes, this was a detached country villa. The only visual concessions to its three story row house neighbors were the concentration of most of its sculpted ornament (in sheet metal and terra-cotta) and a prominent two story bay on the street side of the building. Balancing this bay, in typical Edelmann fashion, were two brick pilasters capped by fanned lotuses framing two flat arched windows with an ornate lunette above. Edelmann's influence is also evident in the prominent slate batter at the base of the frame walls of the second floor. This detail appears in no other building with which Sullivan's name is associated, but Edelmann would employ it even more prominently in the Branford High School (Pl. 28.) he designed nine years later.

The client's specific requirements, rather than contemporary convention, obviously dictated the house's arrangement. To take advantage of the relatively large site, most of the main rooms were oriented toward the large side yard which extended southward to the street corner. Even the main entrance was near the center of the side facade and could only be reached from the street by way of a long veranda also oriented in the direction of the side yard. Most unusual was the positioning of the obligatory front parlor and adjoining library across the front of the house. As if the owner had little use for these ceremonial rooms, a large entrance hall and main staircase cut across the full width of the building, quite effectively isolating them from his actual living space, the rooms of the main floor which faced the yard. Although a substantial portion of the second floor exterior walls was of frame construction, the owner seems to have had an inordinate concern for making sure that at least the first floor would be as fire resistant as cost would allow. All the partitions between the first floor rooms were substantial brick walls, and in an obvious effort to keep flammable wood trim to a minimum, very narrow wood casings were used at all the openings. Not only did such narrow casings never appear in any of Adler & Sullivan's other early residential buildings; but they were also unique for the time.

For most of the same reasons, the Barbe Residence is as easily attributable to Edelmann as the McCormick Residence, but whereas the McCormick followed no particular stylistic precedent, the influence of the American Queen Anne is quite noticeable in the Barbe in the false half timbering and the slate facing of the walls at the second floor. Since Adler & Sullivan continued to rely on that style long after Edelmann had left the firm, it seems reasonable to conclude that this was Sullivan's contribution to the design.

If ever an example were needed to prove that not all the work which came out of the office of Adler & Sullivan in its early years was designed by either principal or their foreman, it is the Mannheimer Residence (extant, 2147 N. Cleveland Avenue, Chicago). Even though it is reminiscent of the McCormick Residence, its ornament and general composition so crudely parody Edelmann and Sullivan's work that it could only have been the creation of one of the firm's junior draftsmen.

While Edelmann chafed under the rule of his former pupil, Sullivan must have been equally irked to be constantly reminded that Edelmann had once shared Adler's confidence and might one day regain it at his expense. When Sullivan detailed his first three dimensional ornaments for Adler on the Borden Block and Rothschild Store, he was already familiar with Edelmann's ornamental style and apparently gave little thought to the potential consequences of continuing to use it in Adler's service. With Edelmann back, Sullivan's failure to have already moved on to something else could only have been a constant reminder to him and Adler of the authority Edelmann continued to hold over him. As if to show Adler that neither partner really needed Edelmann, Sullivan began to abandoned Edelmann's ornamental style as soon as he was gone. From then on, Sullivan would cut himself off from any reference in his architecture which might be creditable to Edelmann. One might conclude, therefore, that this was the primary impetus which led Sullivan to immediately undertake the serious search for his own expression that five years later culminated in the emergence of his mature style in the Wainwright Building in St. Louis.

Little is known about where Edelmann was or what he was doing during most of 1885 and on into 1887. Contrary to what Narciso Menocal has said, Edelmann could not have been involved in Adler & Sullivan's Chicago Auditorium project because he left the firm over a year before it began.[111] It does not seem to have been until 1887 that Edelmann left the Chicago area to permanently settle in the New York area.

Still remaining from Adler & Sullivan's early work is a three house row built for Mrs. Ann Halsted in Chicago in 1884 (1826-30 N. Lincoln Park West). Although the center house features two prominent terra-cotta ornaments applied to the facade in much the same way that Edelmann had inserted one of his fanned lotuses into the front of the Kaufmann Store and

---

[111] Robert Twombley & Narciso G. Menocal: *Louis Sullivan, The Poetry of Architecture*, p.91.

Flats, careful examination reveals that the only feature these have in common with Edelmann's device is their profile which in each case frames a plant form totally unrelated to Edelmann's lotus. That Sullivan had used this profile, although at a much reduced scale (on occasion in precisely the same way) ever since he began working for Adler suggests not only that Sullivan was primarily responsible for the design of this row, but that he was again using the opportunity to parody one of Edelmann's favorite motifs. Nevertheless, a square plaster ceiling escutcheon from the interior of one of the units (Pl. 45.) so clearly resembles the cover of the Guy Perkins Alphabet Book and the borders on Edelmann's presentation drawings that there can be no doubt that he was not only responsible for this detail, but that he played at least some role in this project.

On August 8, 1885, the *American Architect* announced that Mrs. Halsted had obtained a building permit to extend the building two units further north. No mention was made of an architect for this addition. By then Edelmann was no longer working for Adler & Sullivan. Unlike the original building, the ornament of this addition (Pl. 24.) conforms precisely to prototypes which Edelmann had already developed, particularly its fanned lotuses. They are, therefore, unlikely to have been the work of any author other than Edelmann himself. Since the lily is central in the crest of the Lilienthals, the noble line from which Edelmann descended, the replacement of the familiar lotus blossom with a lily seems to have been an effort on Edelmann's part to 'sign' the work. He must, therefore, have taken this client and her commission with him when he left Adler & Sullivan.

In my youth, while driving around Chicago's North Side in the summer of 1960, Richard Nickel took me to see a duplex flat building he had photographed a few months before (Pl. 25.) because he thought that I might find its distinct resemblance to some of Adler & Sullivan's early residential work as interesting to me as it was to him. To verify whether it was theirs, we immediately drove to City Hall, where using this building as an example and taking detailed notes, he taught me how to conduct a title search. When we discovered that the building had very likely been erected as late as 1887, we concluded that it was just too late to be their work. About a year or two later, he told me that it had been demolished. By the time Tim Samuelson and I concluded it could only have been Edelmann's work, Nickel had died. In spite of the remarkable thoroughness with which he had generally documented his research, nothing regarding this building, except for his photographs of it, has yet been found among his papers. Alas, I have searched my memory and numerous insurance maps of both Chicago's North and West Sides, but too many years have passed, and not even I, who saw it, have yet been able to find it again.

No longer forced to kowtow to Sullivan's picturesque preferences, in this building Edelmann returned to a more rational, Eidlitz-like design approach, where the facade clearly expressed the functional and structural divisions of the building behind it. Prominent pilasters with substantial battered bases (like those on the Sinai Temple and the Gilman Building) mark the position of all the transverse bearing walls. To express the essentially similar arrangement of each of its two floors, single flat arched windows were set between each pier, identical to those which Edelmann had already used on the front of the Barbe Residence. A wood porch, complete with spindled gables of the same type used on the Frank, McCormick and Barbe residences, was attached to the front of the building. Ornament was concentrated at the roof line on two differently patterned relief pediments from the top of which sprang a finial composed of four by now very familiar spear shaped leaves. The repeating overlapping "9"-shaped leaf motif at the bottom of the left pediment (Pl. 44.b., no detailed view of the other exists) is precisely the same motif which had already appeared in the segmental pediments of both the Blackstone and Wilshire buildings and the third floor tympanum of the Knisely Store and Flats. If, however, there is anything in this building which might be traceable back to the time Edelmann spent with Adler & Sullivan, it seems to be the delicacy of the ornament which is more like Sullivan's than his earlier work. This appears to have been the last building Edelmann designed using the ornamental motifs and compositional devices he and Sullivan had been employing since 1880. After he moved to the New York area, in mid-1887, he would abandon everything related to that form of architectural expression in favor of a decidedly Richardsonian approach.

CHAPTER 6 - EPILOGUE: NEW YORK 1887-1900

There can be no doubt that for a number of years prior to his death John Edelmann was a fervent supporter of Henry George's ideas on taxation. In *The Autobiography*, Louis Sullivan, however, claims that Edelmann began to vociferously express this interest as early as 1878 while he was working for Burling & Adler. This seems unlikely given the history of George's movement. Sullivan's remarks, however, have long been used in support of the presumption that Edelmann moved to New York in 1886 to participate in Henry George's unsuccessful campaign for mayor of that year.[112] Although Edelmann himself may have propagated this as a way of establishing long standing credentials among his politically radical associates in later years, extensive research by Paul Sprague into George's 1886 campaign revealed no connection whatever with Edelmann.[113] A John H. Edelmann is, however, listed as a secretary in *Trow's New York City Directory* for 1886, but not in either of the same directories for 1885 or 1887. That George's campaign did not begin until late September 1886, roughly five months after the directory entries were compiled would seem to further confirm that if this is our John Edelmann, he was in New York for reasons other than participating in George's campaign. That a duplex flat building was erected in Chicago according to Edelmann's design as late as 1887, and the Cleveland directory does not note the removal of his mother (who accompanied him in his two previous moves) to New York until August 1888 seems to suggest that even if he had been in New York in early 1886, he did not move there permanently until the summer of 1887.

The idea, which has been put forth by others, that Edelmann left Chicago for New York to escape the hunt for subversives which followed the Haymarket Riot of May 4, 1886 is also unfounded. Not only may he have been living in New York at that moment, but his name does not appear in any contemporary accounts or police records in connection with that event. In her memoir *Living My Life*, Emma Goldman states that her involvement in the anarchist cause started with the execution of the Haymarket Riot "conspirators." Although she speaks highly of Edelmann, her failure to recognize him as even a peripheral participant in that event or those which followed seems to further prove that he was not involved in either.[114]

---

[112] Louis H. Sullivan, *The Autobiography of an Idea*, pp. 251-252. *Progress and Poverty*, the book where George first made his tax proposals, was not published until 1879, and the term "single tax," which Sullivan claimed Edelmann used in 1878, did not become current until 1888.

[113] Letter from Paul Sprague to Donald Egbert, July 25, 1965.

[114] Emma Goldman, *Living My Life*, vol. 1, pp. 110, 178 & 189.

It seems more likely that it was again the prospect of work, rather than any political considerations which caused Edelmann to move to New York. In a letter he wrote from Brooklyn on January 30, 1888 to his former client J. B. Perkins in Cleveland requesting a letter of endorsement for an unidentified church project, Edelmann noted, "I have as yet—only one good building in New York City."[115] That first building was the Riverside Baptist Church, and the church project was The Gospel Tabernacle complex which was built to house the various activities and organizations conducted under the leadership of its pastor Dr. Albert B. Simpson (which in 1897 were all merged to form the still active Christian and Missionary Alliance). It may be merely coincidence, but it seems likely that Edelmann's former partner Joseph S. Johnson (who had moved on from architecture into evangelism as a profession around this time) suggested he go to New York to pursue these projects. Edelmann would have been particularly well qualified for them. Not only had he already designed a synagogue and several churches, but as one of the designers of both the Moody Tabernacle and the Central Music Hall in Chicago, he was particularly qualified to design a large, multiuse religious building such as that which Dr. Simpson was planning to build.

The building permit for the Riverside Baptist Church had been applied for in November 1887. By October 13, 1888, construction had progressed far enough for the corner stone to be laid, and by February 10, 1889, services were held for the first time in the partially completed building.[116] It would not be until 1895, however, that the building was finally completed under the direction of architect William E. Bloodgood, a member of the church. Since a photograph of the building (Pl. 27.) reveals no noticeable change in detail from grade to roof, it may be concluded that either Bloodgood was only responsible for interior work, or if he did any exterior work, he remained particularly faithful to the intent of the original design. In none of Edelmann's other buildings were the various functions of the its parts so clearly reflected on the exterior as here. Whether or not Leopold Eidlitz would have approved of its peculiarities, the design appears to have conformed to his concept of "organic" architecture. The entrance was expressed by prominent arches at either side of an ornately domed vestibule at the corner, whose resemblance to an Early Christian baptistry may also have had intended symbolic value. The auditorium was identifiable not only by its half octagon shape but by its massive arched windows, and vertical access was expressed by a stair tower at the east end of the 92nd Street front. The prominent pilasters of

---

[115] Letter among the J. B. Perkins papers at the Western Reserve Historical Society.

[116] *The Record and Guide*, November 19, 1887; *The New York Times*, October 14, 1888, February 11, 1889.

Edelmann's earlier work were still there as well as the arched balustrade of the cornice, which he had first used on the Sinai Temple, but his decision to employ a version of the Richardsonian Romanesque for this project and the later Gospel Tabernacle necessitated the abandonment of the elaborate surface ornament which had been so characteristic of that work. In 1916, this church was replaced by another when the congregation was absorbed into the Central Baptist Church which today occupies the site.

It becomes clear when reviewing the surviving documents related to the construction of The Gospel Tabernacle that the project went through a lengthy planning process, which even the client described as, "months and almost years of prayerful study." Although Edelmann infers in his letter to Perkins that he had completed the final design by the beginning of 1888, it was not until the following September that the church's Trustees were ready to report to their membership that the site had actually been purchased and it was not until January 12, 1889 that it was reported that the cornerstone had been laid and the, "side walls were already carried above the cornerstone."[117] If Edelmann was in New York at the beginning of 1886, it seems far more likely that he was there to consult as an expert with the Trustees on the requirements, which this large complex would have to meet rather than for any political reason. The need for secrecy in as volatile a real estate market, as New York was even then, may explain why Edelmann would have been referred to as a secretary rather than what he really was.

To carry both of these projects out, Edelmann had entered into partnership with Lyndon P. Smith to form the firm of Edelmann & Smith, Architects.[118] That the permit for the Riverside Church had been applied for by November 1887 establishes that the working drawings for it had already been completed. Since it is unlikely that it would have taken two men more than three months to complete them, this would seem to further confirm that Edelmann did not move to the New York area or enter into the partnership until the summer of 1887. Smith, who was eleven years Edelmann's junior, was born in Brooklyn and was still apparently living there with his parents when they met. As both the building permit for the church and Edelmann's letter to Perkins confirm,

---

[117] *The Christian Alliance*, September 1888, February 1889.

[118] Little is known of Lyndon P. Smith. He was apparently born in Brooklyn in 1863. Although his name appears in the Census of 1870 and again in 1880 as the child of William P. Smith, a Stockbroker, by 1900, the family seems to have fallen on hard times. His father is then the only member of it listed in the Census and then as an "Inmate" of a poor house. Although Lyndon Smith is listed throughout the 1890s and early 1900s at various addresses in New York directories, the absence of his name in any locality in the four Censuses conducted in 1900 through 1930, suggests that he either died before 1910 or deliberately was avoiding the Census takers.

for roughly the first year or so of the firm's existence, it was stationed in Brooklyn.

The still extant "L" shaped Gospel Tabernacle complex (now secularized) originally consisted of three distinct but attached structures. Four stories of rooms for Dr. Simpson's Missionary College above a floor of stores and the entrance to the church fronted onto the east side of Eighth Avenue, between 43rd and 44th Streets. A six story hostel, called the Berachah Home, fronted onto 44th Street. Concealed behind both of these and connecting them was the two and a half story church auditorium, which extended straight back from the Eighth Avenue front.[119]

The complex was, therefore, comparable both in size and in function to Johnston & Edelmann's Moody Tabernacle of 1873. The similarity of its oval shaped auditorium (lit from above by an octagonal skylight above a well glazed clerestory) to that of the Moody Tabernacle is obvious. In the intervening years, however, Edelmann had learned the principles of good acoustical design from Dankmar Adler which had made his theater designs already noteworthy in the days when the two were working together. Not only did the main axis of the seating cut transversely across the width of the room to bring the audience closer to the speakers platform, but the seating was arranged on a particularly steep rake in accordance with John Scott Russell's then well known "isacoustic curve," which Alder regarded as essential for good acoustical design.

The presence of most of Edelmann's preferred compositional devices (vertically paired fenestration elements, masonry framed dormers in its mansard roof and coursed stone piers with battered bases framing the ground floor openings) on the main front facing Eighth Avenue, as well as his published perspective of it (Pl. 26.) confirm that this part of the project was primarily his. Compared to the buildings of comparable size he had designed since 1880, it was, like the Riverside Baptist Church, far more restrained. Gone now were both the pilasters and lavish ornamental details of that earlier work. The result was a building which had much more in common with his simpler, more massive work of the 1870s and for which its Richardsonian elements were most congenial. Here again, as in his design for the proposed Englewood church of 1875, this design, though not remarkable for New York at the time, seems to anticipate the work of the Dutch architect H. P. Berlage. Unfortunately this front was completely removed when a story was added to this part of the complex in 1925, but the auditorium itself (now with

---

[119] I am indebted to Christopher Neville and Jenn Whiteman, Archivist of the Christian and Missionary Alliance, who provided me with substantial information on The Gospel Tabernacle.

it main floor leveled off and functioning as part of a pizza restaurant) remains otherwise intact.

. Here the functions of the various spaces behind his facade were again clearly expressed. Not only were the main entrance and commercial spaces on the ground floor defined by cast iron and cut stone construction, but the tower and smaller fenestration elements below it gave a clear indication as to where the access stairs were. The "College Hall" which occupied the second floor was distinguished from the floors above by prominent arched openings and an oriole. The two more plainly treated floors above were apparently occupied by classrooms. The randomly spaced fenestration and mansard of the top floor suggests that it served some function distinct from those below, but what that was is not specified in any of the known descriptions of the building. The executed building differed from Edelmann's perspective only in the addition of another dormer at the right end of the mansard and an increase in the width of all the dormer windows to match those in the tower. These modifications improved the design significantly.

The upper four floors of the six story front of the former Berachah Home at 258-260 West 44th Street is the only part of the exterior of the complex which is still mostly intact, although its ornamental details have for the most part been either removed or covered over. The complexity and misalignment, however, of its various elements is totally alien to any of Edelmann's work and, therefore, must have been Lyndon Smith's contribution to the project. This is confirmed by a crude drawing of the elevation, obviously not in Edelmann's hand, and the published perspective and plans of this part of the building which were published in the dedication issue of *The Christian Alliance and Missionary Weekly* of March 7-14, 1890, which bear the full name of each of the design partners in such a way that Lyndon Smith would have been able to take unquestioned credit for it.

Except for the 1886 listing already referred to, Edelmann's name does not appear in any New York directory until 1889 when his partnership with Lyndon Smith was first acknowledged. When The Gospel Tabernacle was completed in 1890, the partnership was dissolved, which suggests that it existed solely for the purpose of building the two churches. In 1891 and 92, Edelmann was listed as an architect on his own.[120]

What further relationship Edelmann may have had with Lyndon Smith after The Gospel Temple project may never be known, but from 1893 to 1897 he lived in Forest Hill, New Jersey, where Edelmann himself had lived from 1891 to 1893. Whether he moved into Edelmann's former abode, we

---

[120] Dennis Steadman Francis, *Architects in Practice New York City 1840-1900*, p. 28 & p. 70.

may never know. In 1899, Smith, who had just received the commission to design the Bayard Building in Manhattan, sought out Louis Sullivan to design its principal facade. Almost from the beginning Sullivan was given credit as the building's architect with Smith relegated to the position of an associate architect. It seems unlikely that Smith would have accepted such treatment had it not been for the relationship which each had with John Edelmann.

The first time it can be documented that Edelmann participated in any form of political activity was when he spoke as having once been a "Western farmer" in support of the re-election of Grover Cleveland as President, which was hardly a radical position, at a meeting of the Anti-Poverty Society in the Cooper Union on May 13, 1888.[121] As the Gospel Tabernacle was nearing completion, Edelmann, however, appears to have begun to experience what we would today call a mid-life crisis. Prior to then his involvement in church work, particularly his two recent churches, indicates that he adhered to ideas no more radical than those of the popular Social Gospel as espoused by such preachers as Moody and Simpson. Such projects would certainly never have been awarded to anyone espousing the anti religious views of the more extreme socialists and anarchists that he began to associate with, when by May 1891, he had moved to Forest Hill, New Jersey. A year later, he entered into a common law marriage with Rachelle Krimont, a Jewish woman almost half his age.[122] The 1900 Census states that she was born in Russia in September 1870. According to her son, the two met at a Single Tax rally for Henry George.[123]

In 1893, probably because of the imminent arrival of his first child, John W. Edelmann (who was born in June of that year at Forest Hill), Edelmann built a house for himself and his family at 30 Alpine Place, then part of North Arlington, New Jersey, but now part of the adjoining community of Kearney. Although its front has been significantly altered over the years, this modest two and a half story frame house still stands in well maintained condition. Its half gambrel roof, running parallel to the front, was obviously inspired by the then popular Dutch colonial style. In spite of what may not have been an amicable departure from Adler & Sullivan and the hundreds of miles that separated them, Sullivan and Edelmann maintained their friendship. When the house was completed, Sullivan sent the Edelmanns a plaster frieze of a design he had developed for the Wainwright Tomb in St. Louis, which they installed just below the ceiling of the entire living room. Three years later, a daughter,

---

[121] *The New York Times*, May 14, 1888.

[122] Information provided by Henry Bruhl, related to the Krimont side of the family. The 1900 Census confirms the year of their marriage.

[123] Joseph Carter, Editor, *Labor Lobbyist, The Autobiography of John W. Edelmann*, p. 8.

Sonia, was born. By July 1, 1899 (as the New York directory compiled by that date confirms) financial troubles had compelled Edelmann to give up the house and move back to New York.[124]

After The Gospel Tabernacle, Edelmann's interest in architecture waned. From then on he seems to have regarded his chosen profession as merely a means of earning a living. This he expressed in 1892 not only in the title but throughout the text of his only known published work on architecture, *Pessimism of Modern Architecture*.[125] There he describes American architecture as advancing along, "two lines—scholarship and invention." The only exponent of the former he cites is Stanford White. He describes the, "Giralda Tower," of White's Madison Square Garden as, "a work of art, complete and harmonious—not a slavish reproduction in form and spirit—a piece of old Spain transplanted to America." Without actually finding fault with it, he nevertheless saw it as, "an exotic not rooted in our soil, giving only negative expression to American ideas." Its expression may not have been what he thought America needed, but he was at least willing to accept its esthetic merit. Ironically, for an architect who consistently endeavored to be inventive in the 1880s, he was not so polite to the school of "invention." He describes "the works of those who strive for originality, who dream of an 'American style' to be presently invented," as, "infinitely more crude." Although Richardson and Sullivan could obviously be considered proponents of that school, Edelmann refers to the work of Richardson and his followers as an, "authoritative American Expression," and to Sullivan as having in his opinion, "an even deeper insight than Richardson and greater power of expression." While extolling the virtue of the sheer verticality of the fenestration of Sullivan's Wainwright Building and proclaiming it, "one of the masterpieces of architecture," he nevertheless said:

> "Here a great problem is solved. Commercial architecture is revealed,
> no longer a thing of shreds and patches and shams, but direct and
> complete in itself—an embodiment of truth—of most sinister aspect."

---

[124] A $4,250 mortgage on the property issued to, "Rachelle Edelmann, wife of John H. Edelmann of Forest Hill," was recorded by the Hudson County Registrar on October 26, 1893. A deed was subsequently issued by the Edelmanns to Henry G. Greene, the owner of the land, on April 1, 1895. Apparently in exchange for paying off two mortgages (one for $2,000 and another held by Greene for $1,500) which the Edelmanns had apparently gotten to build the house. they were still allowed to reside on the property even though they no longer held title to it.

[125] *The Engineering Magazine*, April 1892, pp. 44-54.

Regarding Adler & Sullivan's thirty four story Fraternity Temple project, he states "to say that the expression is pessimistic is to express an obvious truth, and this despite the fact that the highest skill has been brought to the task." For Edelmann the skyscraper was an essentially inhumane commercial edifice. Even when expressed in the most logical and artistic terms, it was still "sinister." A century later, smog choked cities, "towering infernos" and "9-11" seem to have proven him right. As to his own attitude to his profession he says,

> "If this is to be our future in architecture, well may we regret our rude and buoyant youth, ere we had brought accomplishment, high aims and subtle insight to the service of the prevailing money cult."

Even though Edelmann expressed the view that the, "great artist embodies in his work . . . his own personality, his own ideals," which was at the heart of everything Sullivan stood for, the tone of the article reveals that Edelmann no longer shared Sullivan's dream of an "American style" emerging in the near future. He was right. When Sullivan's work finally began to achieve universal acclaim in the 1930s, it was as the most vital expression of a bygone age, not a blueprint for the future. By the time that happened, the "International Style" had doomed any thought of developing an indigenous architecture. Today, more books are published in America on Sullivan's disciple Frank Lloyd Wright than on any other architect, but at the same time virtually no one is emulating his architecture. The "infinitely more crude" school of "invention" has triumphed. Edelmann hoped that a "great artist's soul" might one day transform the "childish, brutal, vulgar designs" of the followers of that school into a "true national architecture," but over a century later that has yet to happen. Today American architects seem to have either run out of ideas, or resorted to gimmickry as the sole way of being inventive. That brief moment in the late 1880s and early 90s when Richardson's Romanesque took hold of the American imagination was to be the last flowering of anything that had pretensions to becoming an American national style.

In spite of its brevity and lack of exhaustive analysis, Edelmann's *Pessimism of Modern Architecture* may be one of the most prophetic of all nineteenth century architectural writings. His concluding assessment of architecture is that, "the world over the old joyous art is dead . . . and from modern commercialism no happy art can spring." These were views which had already been expressed by Eidlitz in *The Nature and Function of Art*. They are even more true now than they were then.

Edelmann's pessimism toward his profession is particularly evident in the buildings he designed soon after he had established himself in New York. While some of the Riverside Baptist Church's peculiar features could still have been regarded as somewhat "innovative," the two fronts of The Gospel Tabernacle complex confirm that he had already abandoned the exoticisms of his work both in Chicago and in Cleveland of the 1880s in favor of a more subdued approach. The Decker Building in New York begun in 1892, which he reputedly designed for architect Alfred Zucker; the home he designed and built for his family at North Arlington (now Kearney), and the small, no longer extant, four classroom Branford High School (Pl. 28. later the Laurel Street School) in Branford, Connecticut which he designed in 1894,[126] are all typical examples of the eclecticism of their day. In the Decker Building, Moorish and Venetian Gothic elements are indiscriminately combined. Even its client driven ornamental excesses essentially accord with those styles. Rather than adopt what he had already acknowledged to be Sullivan's successful solution for the architectural problem of the skyscraper, Edelmann apparently remained wedded to his old habits. Just as he had done in The Gospel Tabernacle facades, the fenestration patterns of this ten story building extend through no more than two floors, thus negating any expression of its height. The Branford school was only slightly less eclectic. For the most part it was a competent but uninspired example of the Colonial Revival style of the day complete with a Tuscan-columned front porch and Palladian windows. Its asymmetrical appearance at first glance suggest that Edelmann was still employing Eidlitz's approach to planning, but the very slight variation in the dimensions of the classrooms on either side of its central hallway suggest that this was really driven by a desire for asymmetry rather than functional necessity. These five buildings and the interiors of the Hotel Majestic in New York, completed in 1894, which Edelmann also reputedly designed for Zucker, are the only works designed after Edelmann left Chicago which have so far been attributed to him.

Although Edelmann's efforts on behalf of the anarchist cause gleaned him some notoriety, they led nowhere.[127] Emma Goldman's first mention of Edelmann in her autobiography as a "publicist" obviously refers to his involvement with the publication of the anarchist journal *Solidarity*. In 1892 he began contributing to it, and a year later he and his friends took over its publication, but lack of funds forced it to suspend publication several times.

---

[126] Information provided by Paul Sprague

[127] The general tone of his political speeches and the response they received was noted in the following: *The New York Time*s, May 7,1894; November 12, 1894; March 18, 1895.

Following a final infusion of funds in 1897 from Prince Peter Kropotkin, the noted Russian anarchist (who stayed with the Edelmanns while making an American tour) it was forced to permanently cease publication.[128] Goldman's two other references to him are in connection with a revival of *Solidarity* in 1894 and as a member of a committee organized to fight the reemergence of the Inquisition in Spain. From her often repeated references to other anarchists and the little she had to say about Edelmann, it is certain that Goldman did not regard him as a major figure in the anarchist movement.

From June 1896 through December 1897, Edelmann was employed by McKim, Mead and White as a sculptor doing interior work on their Library for New York University.

In 1898, he went back into private practice while still doing work for others. Most of this other work appears to have been as a construction superintendent. On July 12, 1900, while apparently superintending the construction, ". . . of the mansion in Fifth Avenue which is being built for William A. Clark, of Montana, the millionaire mine owner and ousted Senator," John Edelmann died.[129] The most thorough account of his death appears to have been that in *The New York Herald* the next day where it states:

> "[he] died suddenly yesterday presumably of heat prostration, at No. 142 Fifth Avenue. A few hours earlier he had closed his home at No. 8 West 102nd Street for the summer and sent his family to Long Branch.
>
> Mr. Edelman (sic!) had been to see Thomas J. Reilly, a builder, upon a matter of business and started to return to his office about four o'clock. He was taken ill in the elevator car and swooned when the ground floor was reached. An ambulance was summoned from the New York Hospital, but when it arrived Dr. Kenyon found that Mr. Edelman was dead.
>
> The body was taken to the morgue."

The record of his cremation at the Fresh Pond Crematorium in Middle Village, New York cites his occupation as that of "Draughtsman" and confirms that he died on July 12 of "Insolation" (sun or heatstroke) at 142 Fifth Avenue.[130] According to personnel of the Fresh Pond Crematorium, his ashes

---

[128] "In Search of John Edelmann, Architect and Anarchist," *A. I. A. Journal*, February 1966, p. 41.

[129] Unidentified obituary, copy provided by Paul Sprague

[130] The United States Cremation Co.'s "Application for Incineration No. 3664" further states that Edelmann's body was cremated on Saturday July 14, 1900

were not deposited in their columbarium. Their records indicate only that they were turned over to the undertaker on July 16, 1900.

No longer able to rely on her son for support and without any willingness on the part of his wife to continue it, Edelmann's mother (who had been living with him and his family throughout his New York years) returned to Cleveland to live with relatives.[131] Throughout Edelmann's forty-seven years of life, he lived with her for all but eleven years (1872 to mid-1876 and 1881 to mid-1887), and of those years, three had been spent living near her and the Bluims when he returned to Cleveland in the 1880s. Her attachment to him, which was apparently reciprocated, seems obvious. It seems possible, therefore, that she may have taken the ashes of her beloved son with her when she returned to Cleveland.[132]

Following Edelmann's death, his widow suffered a nervous breakdown. While this was undoubtedly precipitated by the shock of his sudden death, the circumstances of their marriage suggest that the underlying cause was more likely having to live for eight years with a despondent husband and his elderly mother. Her mother-in-law was a Christian and apparently a member of the minor German nobility. Her son's "paperless" marriage to a Jewish woman of Russian birth, roughly half his age, who belonged to the kind of radical political movement she and Edelmann's father had come to America to avoid, must have been a source of constant friction between the two women. Add to that his wife's youth, the loss of their home in New Jersey, Edelmann's pessimistic attitude toward life and his failure to achieve any lasting success in his chosen profession, and there can be no doubt that the pressures of the marriage on her must have been considerable.

Roughly six months after Edelmann's death, his wife and their children went to England to live with her brother, Senia Krimont. Almost immediately after their arrival, she entered a sanitarium in Brighton. A year later, she gathered her children up and moved to the utopian Whiteway Colony, where she soon married William Sinclair, one of the leaders of the colony.[133] After

---

[131] Interview with Edelmann's daughter, Sonia Clements, as reported in a letter from Donald Egbert to Paul Sprague of May 31, 1965. The 1900 Census indicates that Edelmann's mother was still living with her son and his family just before his death.

[132] Drew Rolik has reported that he was unable to find any record of her burial or that of her son's ashes in either the Monroe Cemetery, where her husband was buried, or the Lake View Cemetery where the Bluims are buried nor could he find her name in any Cleveland directories from 1898 to 1907

[133] Joseph Carter, Editor, *Labor Lobbyist, The Autobiography of John W. Edelman*, pp. 1-14). For those interested in his father, this autobiography is disappointing. Although he provided Egbert and Sprague with many useful reminiscences of his father and his childhood in America, his book provides almost none of that information.

Sinclair died in 1929, she returned to America to live with her family. At the time of her death in 1952, she was living with her son in Virginia.

While still living in England when World War I began, Edelmann's son dropped the last "n" in the family name. He returned to America in 1916 and eventually became a prominent labor lobbyist. His daughter remained in England for the rest of her life.

Looking back at Edelmann's life roughly a quarter century after his death, Sullivan had this to say in *The Autobiography*, about his friend Edelmann's outlook on life as compared to his own:

> "Louis soon noticed that he himself had a clear program in life, John had none. That all this talk, while of deep import to him, was for John merely luxurious self-indulgence and a luscious hour with parade of vanity; that he, the elder, regarded the younger with patronage, much as a bright child, but a tyro in the active world; while Louis saw that John was merely drifting. In this regard each kept his thoughts to himself, while encouraging the other."[134]

As harsh as it is, this assessment seems just. From the beginning, Sullivan recognized that architecture was just as much a business as an art, which required an architect to have a sufficient number of wealthy patrons if he was to be very successful. He knew that his own low status in what Edelmann called "the social order" would be an impediment to acquiring such a clientele. Sullivan's "program in life," therefore, consisted of following through on the most obvious shortcut around this otherwise potentially insurmountable problem. He would endeavor to find a, "middle aged architect of standing, with the right sort of clientele," and, "make himself so indispensable that partnership would naturally follow," and that is what he did after Edelmann introduced him to Dankmar Adler.[135]

Edelmann may have understood the nature of "the social order" but throughout his career he chose to ignore its realities much to his own misfortune. Therein alone, despite his diverse talents, may be found the source of his failure to achieve any prominence in his chosen profession or in politics. The evidence confirms that his habit of "drifting" from city to city and from employer to employer in search of work not only prevented him from remaining in any place long enough to find permanent patronage, but when he did temporarily settle down, he generally preferred rural suburban

---

[134] Louis H. Sullivan, *The Autobiography of an Idea*, pp. 208-209.
[135] Louis H. Sullivan, *The Autobiography of an Idea*, p. 251.

environments far away from the central city, where he would have been far more likely to have found patronage. Of the roughly fourteen years he lived in the New York area, most of them were spent living in suburban New Jersey. He is only known to have lived in Manhattan in the last year of his life and then reluctantly. Edelmann's indulgence in the use of avant-garde Victorian Gothic and Dresser forms in his early work did impress and have a profound effect upon his apprentice Sullivan, but the course of his work indicates that it was in the end one aspect of Edelmann's architecture which Sullivan might rightly have called, "merely luxurious self-indulgence and a . . . parade of vanity." By 1890, two thirds of the way through his professional career, Edelmann had become disillusioned with the future of architecture, as his *Pessimism of Modern Architecture* confirms. As much as he extolled the anarchist cause, his efforts generally fell on deaf ears, and the little press he got for them so further diminished whatever professional reputation he had left that his death certificate and the undertaker in charge of the disposal of his mortal remains both refer to him not as an architect but merely as a "draughtsman." Although the day after his death three other New York newspapers took note of it, their interest was aroused only by its bizarre nature and not who he was, which they barely and often erroneously noted.[136]

---

[136] *The New York Tribune; New York Times*, and *The World. The World* incorrectly noted his age as 55 and that he was architect of the "Auditorium Hotel in Chicago

CHAPTER 7 - JOHN EDELMANN'S INFLUENCE ON LOUIS SULLIVAN AND HIS ARCHITECTURE

With Edelmann's departure from Adler & Sullivan in 1885, his professional relationship with Sullivan came to an end. The history of that relationship does not in itself explain the full nature of the debt Sullivan owed Edelmann. That can only be comprehended through a review of how Sullivan's own work and his understanding of his profession were inspired by Edelmann during those years when they worked together.

In *The Autobiography*, Louis Sullivan gave the following words of praise for John Edelmann's intellect and the effect it had upon him:[137]

> "It gradually dawned upon Louis that he had run across a THINKER, a profound thinker, a man of immense range of reading, a brain of extraordinary keenness, strong, vivid, that ranged in its operations from saturnine intelligence concerning men and their motives, to the highest transcendentalisms of German metaphysics. He was as familiar with the great philosophers as with the daily newspapers. As an immediate psychologist, never before or since has Louis met his equal in vitality, in verity, and in perspicacity of thought. He, John, knew all that the psychologists had written, and much, of his own discernment, that they but recently had begun to unveil . . . .
>
> One day John explained his theory of suppressed functions; and Louis, startled, saw in a flash that this meant the real clue to the mystery that lay behind the veil of appearances. Louis was peculiarly subject to shock from unexpected explosion of a single word; and when the word 'function' was detonated by the word 'suppressed,' a new, an immense idea came suddenly into being and lit up his inner and his outer world as one. Thus, with John's aid, Louis saw the outer and the inner world more clearly, and the world of men began to assume a semblance of form, and of function."

Sullivan went on to speak of Edelmann stimulating his interest in Wagner to the point that he, ". . . became an ardent Wagnerite." In conclusion he summarizes their relationship with the statement, ". . . he [Edelmann] was the benefactor and Louis the parasite and profiteer."

---

[137] Louis H. Sullivan, *The Autobiography of an Idea*, pp. 206-210.

This, however, tells us nothing of what in Sullivan's own architecture he got from Edelmann or his philosophizing except to suggest that his famous dictum, "form follows function," had its origin in Edelmann's, "theory of *suppressed functions*." Unfortunately Sullivan chose not to explain what that theory was.

Both Edelmann and Sullivan entered the architectural profession at a time when any building contractor could use the title, "Architect," and be accepted as such. The amazing achievements of both civil and structural engineers, particularly in the construction of bridges and railroads, had caught the imagination of the public, as Sullivan himself testifies in *The Autobiography*. The ever increasing need to enclose large spaces had begun to move the engineer into territory formerly reserved for the architect alone. The older generation of architects, those active before the Civil War, seem to have remained oblivious to these currents, but by the 1870s it was becoming evident to the younger generation—like Edelmann and Sullivan—that their profession could no longer compete in the same arena with the engineers. To one degree or another, they would have to become dilettantes, promoters of architecture as an art for art's sake, if the profession was to again receive significant public recognition. The degree to which each of these men accepted the new reality was ultimately shaped by their training.

Although Edelmann's own training was not undertaken in an academic environment, it seems to have followed at least the essence of the German polytechnic system, which would have been well known to his first employer, Alexander Koehler, and his assistants, the Cudell brothers. Koehler most likely began instructing him in construction techniques, while the Cudells then took over his training in the principles of design. Koehler was an architect of the old school, a competent practitioner who, like most of his contemporaries, seems to have regarded the historic styles as merely a source of motifs suitable for decorating properly constructed buildings. By introducing Edelmann to the High Victorian Gothic, the Cudells were able to instill in him a desire to go beyond sound building and achieve some level of artistic innovation. When Edelmann first arrived in Chicago in 1872, the training he had received at the hands of Koehler and the Cudells was more than sufficient to enable him to take charge of work in the offices of both Burling & Adler and W. L. B. Jenney.

Sullivan's reference to Edelmann's understanding of "the highest transcendentalisms of German metaphysics" does, however, raise two questions about his training. How did a man who appears to have had only an elementary school education come to be so knowledgeable about such ideas, and of what importance were they to Sullivan that he would still take note of them roughly fifty years later? In her previously cited monograph on Leopold Eidlitz, Kathryn Holliday demonstrates that Eidlitz's concept of an "organic architecture" was in part based on these same ideas. The obvious affinity of the planning methods of both Eidlitz and Edelmann suggests that these ideas were most likely communicated to him by Eidlitz's former employee Frank Cudell while the two were working for Koehler. Whether Edelmann ever referred to their author when communicating them to Sullivan may never be known, but Sullivan's dictum, "form follows function," and Edelmann's theory of *suppressed functions*, which inspired it, seem to both reflect the importance of function in Eidlitz's concept of "organic architecture." Sullivan's own use of contrasting volumes to occasionally acknowledge functional differences within his buildings was likely a legacy of seeing Edelmann apply Eidlitz's functionalist planning principles. In spite of that, Sullivan's own approach to planning was always far less rigid. The box-like nature of most of his buildings did at least allow for subsequent changes in program.

When they first met, Edelmann had completed his apprenticeship in Koehler's office two years before, and Sullivan was still in the midst of that process. From its onset Sullivan's training was greatly influenced by his academic experiences. He had started out in architecture, not in an architect's office, but as a student at M.I.T. under a Beaux Arts inspired program, which, like its parent, was more interested in the esthetic and planning aspects of architecture, than in structural systems and materials. However, after only a five month stay at the École itself, his search for knowledge there left him unsatisfied. By his own account, the only things he found of value at the École were its planning methods and the status of a dilettante, which it could confer on any American who had been there. The latter was a role he would in time fully exploit. He then returned to Chicago to continue his apprenticeship under Edelmann's more practical tutelage in the office of Johnston & Edelmann.

By 1882, Sullivan had come to regard himself as so much of an esthete that when interviewed about his work on the interior renovation of Hooley's Theatre, the reporter noted that, "Mr. Sullivan is a pleasant gentleman, but somewhat troubled with large ideas tending to metaphysics, and a deprecation of the non-development of the art protoplasm dormant in this city. It is therefore difficult to learn from Mr. Sullivan exactly what he has done." The reporter went on to say that Sullivan wished to have his work described, "as a new phase in the art view of architecture."[138]

The authoritative list of Louis Sullivan's architectural designs, both built and unbuilt, in the 1998 revised edition of Hugh Morrison's *Louis Sullivan,*

---

[138] *Inter Ocean* (Chicago) August 13, 1882

Prophet of Modern Architecture includes 234 entries. This is certainly a lot more work than Edelmann could have ever claimed, but when Sullivan entered Adler's employ things were much different. By that time Edelmann was already responsible for the design of fourteen projects of which eight had actually been built. Dankmar Adler was a very experienced architect when Sullivan replaced Edelmann as his office foreman. He had relied on Edelmann's abilities as a consultant architect off and on for roughly eight years. Sullivan is not known to have designed even one building up to that point. With little experience other than as a designer of two dimensional decorations, Adler was not likely, even with Edelmann's endorsement, to immediately entrust the design of any aspect of a building other than its ornamental embellishment to such an untested individual. It is therefore not surprising that Sullivan would have been responsible only for the ornament on the Borden Block and Rothschild Store which were begun just after he arrived in the office.

The ornament of the Borden Block featured Edelmann's fluted leaves and variations on his spear shaped leaf, but rosettes, which were hallmarks of his work at the time, were barely present. The ornament was, however, much lusher than Edelmann's. and unlike his, there were no blank spaces to form a background.

In the ornament of the Rothschild Store (Pl. 29.), Edelmann's influence was more apparent. The roof cornice featured foliage similar to Edelmann's representation of "the lotus of the Calumet" on the smaller bases of the ground floor piers of the Kimball Building (Pl. 39.).

Following the Rothschild Store until early 1885, when Edelmann had ceased working for Adler & Sullivan, the firm had received roughly sixty commissions. An examination of several key examples show that in spite of the use of the same Edelmann inspired style of ornament, there was no consistency whatever in Sullivan's approach to architectural composition, nor was there much effort on his part to adopt Edelmann's approach to design.

It was not until the spring of 1881, after Sullivan had been working as his office foreman for almost a year, that Adler finally gave him substantial control over the design of two buildings: the S. A. Maxwell & Co. Store (extant, 19 S. Wabash Avenue, Chicago, Pl. 30.) and the A. S. Gage & Co. Store,[139] (no longer extant, northeast corner of Wabash Avenue and Adams Street, Chicago). The results of this decision were far from impressive. The structural systems Adler had employed in the Borden Block and Rothschild

---

[139] Although this building was said to be, "fire proof," its floors were supported entirely by combustible wood joists to which terra-cotta fireproofing tiles were nailed.

Store had determined the arrangement of their architectural features. These buildings were to be of basically the same construction, but at this stage in his career, Sullivan obviously regarded a concern for structural integrity as a hindrance to artistic expression. By deliberately changing the direction of the framing in the front bays so that only the ends of the wood floor joists, the weakest and most combustible part of the structural system, would bear on the front walls, he was able to avoid any reference on the facades to the position of the interior columns. With that need gone, Sullivan could place the cast iron and masonry elements of his facades almost anywhere he wished, and that he did. Years later a fire on the top floor of Adler & Sullivan's Wirt Dexter Building built in 1887, where the same system was used again, would reveal the serious deficiencies of such construction. When the joists burned through, the top floor of the facade collapsed. Although Sullivan was obviously attempting to produce something independent of the work of his two mentors, Adler and Edelmann in these two buildings, both of them, particularly the Maxwell Store, resemble the Royal Phelps and the Paran Stevens buildings in New York, both designed by Richard Morris Hunt in 1872, more than they do any building designed by either Adler or Edelmann.[140]

The next large commission Adler received was the Academy of Music in Kalamazoo, Michigan (no longer extant, 131 S. Rose Street, Pl. 31.) begun in 1881. Adler's most often noted claim to fame was his knowledge of acoustics and theater design. His influence on the design of the interior is therefore predictable, and since this was only the second public hall (the Central Music Hall was the first) where his firm was given the opportunity to design the facade of the building as well, it is unlikely that he would have left it entirely in Sullivan's hands. The substantial pilasters, demarcating the theater entrance from the adjoining commercial wings of the front, hark back to the functional and structural logic of Adler's earlier work. The overall composition of its polychromatic facade was derived from the popular French inspired mansarded work of the day.

More expressive of its structure and functions was the architecturally similar Hammond Library of the Chicago Theological Seminary (no longer extant, 44 N. Ashland Avenue, Pl. 33,) which D. Adler & Co. designed a year later. Despite its small size, as the only entirely noncombustible building that either Adler or Sullivan would design prior to the Chicago Auditorium, it was also the most substantial. As had been the case in the Rothschild Store, its pleasing symmetry was dictated primarily by the uniformly spaced members

---

[140] See photographs in Robert A. M. Stern, Thomas Mellins & David Fishman: *New York 1880*, p. 413 & 716.

of its internal iron framing, which was entirely encased in Peter B. Wight's system of terra-cotta fire proofing. The different functions of the building (reading rooms on the ground floor with a two story grand hall for the stacks above) were clearly expressed on the facade by various architectural devices rendered by Sullivan in an unusually restrained manner. All factors considered, it was Sullivan's most successful design prior to the Auditorium.

Another building, which Sullivan designed for Adler in the same style as these two, was the Nevada Hotel part of the Rosenfeld Building (Pl. 34.) built in 1882. Not only has the similarity of this building to Edelmann's Blackstone-Perkins Power Building of the year before long been noted,[141] but the treatment of its walls also has a marked similarity to those of his Kimball Building.

The radical differences in style between the various residential buildings produced by the firm of Adler & Sullivan when it began has been explained by the involvement of others in their design. We may be sure, however, due to their relatively small number, that whatever stylistic differences may be found in the homes built before the firm came into existence were entirely due to Sullivan's own search for an architectural expression he could call his own. In spite of his continued reliance on Edelmann's ornamental style, almost from the moment he began to work for Adler, Sullivan began distancing himself from Edelmann's approach to architecture. This can be seen in a comparison with the Marx Wineman Residence (no longer extant, 2544 S. Michigan Avenue, Chicago, Pl. 32.), one of the first houses he designed, and Edelmann's Borden Residence. Both were the same height, composed in essentially the same way and made of the same combination of materials, but there the similarity ended. The Wineman Residence's foundation rose straight out of the ground. Its wall planes were broken up into relatively narrow segments by projections and very wide windows. The symmetry of the front was disrupted by a well glazed two story bay at one end. In place of Edelmann's effort to achieve balanced monumentality, Sullivan had substituted exuberant picturesqueness. This was particularly evident in the massive roof crestings and gargantuan volutes of the the porch column capitals.

The Morris Selz Residence (no longer extant, 1717 S. Michigan Avenue, Chicago, Pl. 22.) was most likely designed as Edelmann was beginning to take up his duties as Adler & Sullivan's foreman. Most of its architectural and decorative features seem to have been selected by Sullivan in a deliberate effort to repudiate some of Edelmann's favorite ways of doing things. The front was built mostly of brownstone, but a substantial amount of wood, sheet metal

---

[141] "In Search of John Edelmann," *A.I.A. Journal*, February 1966, pp. 37-38.

and even terra-cotta also went into it. As if to deny the truthful expression of the nature of these materials implied in Edelmann's understanding of "organic architecture", it was given a monochromatic appearance by painting these other materials to imitate not only the color but the texture of the brownstone. This denial of reality was carried further into the details of the veranda, whose thin railings and columns leave the impression of wood, but were in fact also of brownstone. Although Sullivan apparently condescended to allow Edelmann to install one of his fanned lotuses at the roof above the bay, everywhere else, particularly in the entrance vestibule and staircase, this was modified into a significantly different motif. For the first and only time, the fan shaped part of the motif was carried out in the traditional Egyptian manner of a blossom resting on three leaves, almost as if Sullivan was poking fun at Edelmann for not using the lotus blossom in its archeologically correct manner. There is no other residence attributable to Sullivan comparable in appearance to this building. With it, he seems to have established the boundaries within which he expected Edelmann to work and would never again have a reason to go through such a peculiar architectural exercise.

By 1883, Sullivan had begun to show an interest in the prevailing Queen Anne style for his domestic work. The three adjoining houses for Max M. Rothschild (no longer extant, south side of 32nd St. west of Indiana Avenue, Chicago) were probably the first of these buildings. The Queen Anne influence in the contemporary Barbe Residence was most likely provided by Edelmann at Sullivan's behest.

The Ruben Rubel Residence of 1884 (no longer extant, 320 S. Ashland Avenue, Chicago) was one of Sullivan's more unusual experiments. It had much in common with the design he had produced for the Wineman Residence, but the detailing was more original, a mixture of motifs from Renaissance, Rococo and Moorish sources. With the exception of its stone base, Sullivan's apparent intent was to produce another monochromatic design, this time in red brick and terra-cotta. The presence of two miniscule, fanned lotuses in the brickwork of the building's projecting bay establish that Edelmann was involved with this project but only to a minor degree. That Sullivan may actually have experimented with sharing the responsibility of designing some of the ornamental details with Edelmann is suggested by the identical bottom panels of the two front doors where a symmetrical central element was flanked by two totally different motifs.[142] Perhaps each man designed half of it.

---

[142] Linda L. Chapman, Joyce Jackson & David C. Huntley: *Louis H. Sullivan Architectural Ornament Collection Southern Illinois University at Edwardsville*, Fig. 19.

Since the invention of the metal framed skyscraper by Jenney in 1885, it has been generally assumed that such a frame would be required in order to obtain the maximum amount of light through a fire resistant wall. That Adler, among others of the day, had long been able to achieve such openness without resorting to a metal frame may be one reason why it took so long for that technology to emerge. Its need was simply not that apparent. Of the four commercial buildings Adler & Sullivan designed while Edelmann was with the firm, only the architectural treatment of the Scoville Building (no longer extant, 619-31 W. Washington Blvd., Chicago) appears to have been entirely Sullivan's work. The application of this straightforward system of masonry skeletal construction was somewhat compromised by the necessity of repeating the front of an existing building (at the east end of the site) at the other end of its long facade in order to maintain the overall symmetry of the structure, but the expression of a skeletal facade was more clearly expressed in the center part of the main front of this building than in any other structure either Adler or Sullivan would design until well into the 1890s.[143]

As Sullivan worked his way through the gamut of popular styles, he must have gained considerable confidence to realize that Edelmann, the man he had once so idolized, was no more capable of developing something new and unique out of them than he was. Sullivan continued to experiment with these styles for some time after Edelmann was no longer working for him. Eventually, like so many of his contemporaries, he turned for inspiration to the work of H. H. Richardson. However, he never seems to have been interested in developing the kind of vocabulary of architectural forms that define Richardson's architecture and would later define that of his own disciple Frank Lloyd Wright. Even after he moved into what is regarded as his mature style with the Wainwright Building in St. Louis, his skyscraper projects are indiscriminately dominated by either the prevailing bay and "Chicago" windows of his contemporaries, or arches and other motifs treated in either a basically Romanesque or Renaissance fashion.

From the time Sullivan entered the work force as a draftsman in mid-1873 until he replaced Edelmann as Dankmar Adler's office foreman in 1880, only the interior decoration of both the Moody Tabernacle and the Sinai Temple, each done under Edelmann's direction, are known to have been designed by him. In spite of this relatively small volume of work, fifteen drawings by

---

[143] Paul E. Sprague: "Sullivan's Scoville Building, A Chronology," *Prairie School Review*, Third Quarter, 1974.

Sullivan (all for two dimensional decorations) survive from this period.[144] None of them appear to have been copied directly from any known source, but the plant motifs and birds of various kinds that appear in them all have a clear resemblance to those found in the published works of Christopher Dresser, from which Edelmann had also sought inspiration.[145]

The similarity of some sketches by Frank Furness, Sullivan's first employer, to these designs has led some to propose Furness as their source. That argument carries little weight, however, because the Furness sketches used to back it up are as likely to have been derived from Dresser as Sullivan's drawings were.[146] Furness was certainly not above consulting such English sources for his architecture. Even his often highly publicized High Victorian Gothic work is so remarkably similar to the published work of the English "rogue architects" of the previous decade (in particular that of E. Bassett Keeling) that there seems little doubt that he was deliberately emulating them.

Among Sullivan's other drawings from this period are several copied directly from other sources, probably while he was in Paris. In spite of the attention some historians have given to these tracings of Classical details and plates from Ruprich-Robert's *Flore ornementale* not one of them has yet to point out any Sullivan ornament that could have been derived from these sources.[147]

Sullivan may not have found much in Edelmann's architecture worth emulating, but as Irving Pond said, there was something in Edelmann's ornament that "sunk deep into Louis' consciousness and Louis' ornament of the earlier period was little more than an interpretation of these emanations from John," and, "he made them his own." That Edelmann, as Pond claimed, "inoculated" Sullivan into his style of ornament seems impossible to deny. Although a drawing exists which suggests that in 1881 Sullivan may even have played with the idea, he never really accepted the disjointed arrangement

---

[144] All these drawings are illustrated in Paul E. Sprague: *The Drawings of Louis Henry Sullivan* and in Robert Twombley & Narciso G. Menocal: *Louis Sullivan, The Poetry of Architecture*.

[145] Sullivan's use of Dresser wall papers reputedly designed specifically for his Hooley's Theatre renovation of 1882 confirms his early admiration for Dresser's ornamental designs. See *Chicago Evening Journal*, August 12, 1882.

[146] It must be noted that Furness used an ornament remarkably similar to Edelmann's, "Spandrel-synagogue," detail a year later for the spandrels of his Brazilian Pavilion in the Main Building of the 1876 Centennial Exhibition. This suggests that both men were inspired by the same design produced by a third party, possibly Dresser.

[147] In their *Louis Sullivan, The Poetry of Architecture*, Robert Twombley and Narciso G. Menocal presume that the drawings of the Classical Orders were made in 1872 while Sullivan was still at M.I.T. Since these student drawings bear no date and all the legends are in French, it would seem more likely that they were made while he was a student in Paris at the end of 1874 and the beginning of 1875.

of leaf motifs that Edelmann had first used in the Strauss Residence.[148] His own sensibilities required that he arrange his botanical forms as if they were growing out of each other in a natural manner.

That Sullivan is today remembered most as the author of a unique style of ornament does not mean that he was any less an architect. He designed buildings and carried them to completion, but like most of his contemporaries, he was content to allow their general form to be dictated by his client's requirements and the generally available construction techniques of the day. Lacking the engineering background that allowed his disciple Frank Lloyd Wright to be somewhat adventurous with structural innovations, the construction and overall architectural composition of his mature works seldom if ever differed significantly from the more Classically inspired work of many of his contemporaries, such as Holabird & Roche or Howard Van Doren Shaw to name a few. Strip his buildings of their florid ornament and what is left is not substantially different from theirs. Nevertheless, the one thing that does make his work significantly different and the only thing that is consistent about his architecture throughout his career is the progressive evolution of his ornamental style. Given the essentially different stylistic phases which his architecture passed through, it is only the ornament that ties these buildings together as the work of one man. It is, therefore, Sullivan's ornament that primarily defines his architectural style, just as a profusion of acanthus leaves at the top of its columns defines a building as Corinthian or a scroll at the top of otherwise similar columns will define a building as Ionic. Sullivan seems to have recognized this as his greatest achievement because at the end of his life, the one legacy that he wanted to leave to posterity was not a record of his buildings but rather a series of drawings, almost exclusively of ornamental details, going back to the days of his employment with Johnston & Edelmann and the drawings he had just completed for his last published work, *A System of Architectural Ornament, according with a Philosophy of Man's Powers*.

He summarizes the purpose of his almost lifelong obsession with ornament in the first paragraph of this last work:

> "By the word inorganic is commonly understood that which is lifeless,
> or appears to be so; as stone, the metals, and seasoned wood, clay, or
> the like. But nothing is really inorganic to the creative will of man.

---

[148] This drawing dated April 16, 1881 is reproduced in Paul E. Sprague: *The Drawings of Louis Henry Sullivan*, Fig. 13 and in Robert Twombley & Narciso G. Menocal: *Louis Sullivan, The Poetry of Architecture*, Pl. 86. All of the motifs in it are common to Edelmann's work at the time, but the drawing technique is similar to known Sullivan drawings of the time. Since it is not signed, it cannot be confirmed which of the two drew it.

His spiritual power masters the inorganic and causes it to live in forms which his imagination brings forth from the lifeless, the amorphous. He thus transmutes into the image of his passion that which of itself has no such power. Thus man in his power brings forth that which hitherto was non-existent."

There was nothing new in this. The idea that inanimate material could be reshaped by the hand of man to embody some lofty ideal (in this case the very creative power of man) had often been the justification behind changes in style, the Greek and Gothic Revivals to name but a few. Even the remarks of Christopher Dresser that may have influenced Edelmann's ornamental treatment of the Strauss Residence are a form of it. One could even conclude from this that the geometric ornaments of Sullivan's followers, Frank Lloyd Wright and Claude Bragdon, were expressions of his viewpoint, but Sullivan's preference for botanical over geometric forms indicates that his vision was much narrower. By choosing botanical forms he obviously thought that forms taken from life would in themselves make his architecture living or to use his terminology, "organic." The essence of American building technology, which is still based on the assembling of mass produced parts, whether they be two by fours or repeating pieces of ornamental terra-cotta, would mean that no matter what Sullivan did his ornaments would always appear attached to rather than growing out of the walls of his buildings. Sullivan may never have realized the impossibility of achieving his "organic" goal, but he did produce some of the most beautiful architectural ornament that has ever been created. Gaudi and some of the other followers of the Art Nouveau may have been more successful in creating the illusion of organic growth, but it could never be more than an illusion.

As Edelmann and Sullivan were working together for the last time on the design of the temporary Opera Festival Hall, Edelmann could hardly have guessed that within a few short years that project would catapult Adler & Sullivan into a national reputation as architects of the Chicago Auditorium. Had Edelmann stayed with the firm, some of that glory would surely have fallen on him. Unfortunately for him, his decision to leave at that critical moment, over which Sullivan may have given him little choice, would divert his future career into obscurity, which his subsequent rejection of capitalism, as expressed in his *Pessimism of Modern Architecture*, would only compound.

There seem to be two ways of looking at Edelmann's influence on Sullivan. If one expects to find it solely in the composition of Sullivan's buildings, then it must be concluded that he had no influence upon Sullivan at all. On the other hand, if one accepts that Sullivan's architecture is in the end defined by his ornament, one must also accept that by inoculating Sullivan with his own unique vocabulary of ornamental motifs at the beginning of his career and in guiding him in their use, John Edelmann had a greater influence on Sullivan's architecture than any other man. Edelmann alone had provided Sullivan with the tools with which he began his own study of "organic" ornament that would become the passion of his life and the hallmark of his architecture.

With the exception of Irving Pond, who immediately noticed the omission in *The Autobiography* of a just account of Edelmann's role in the evolution of Sullivan's ornament, for over thirty years after Sullivan's death, everyone who wrote about him, including Morrison, was willing to accept its details as fact. It was not until Willard Connelley's *Louis Sullivan as He Lived* was published in 1960 that some of the major omissions in Sullivan's memoir came to light, but Connelley still accepted most of its errors as fact. Since then various researchers have continued to unearth further facts about Sullivan and his various associates. These have revealed *The Autobiography* to be a highly fictionalized memoir.

What then were the real motives behind Sullivan's failure to even recognize Edelmann as an architect, let alone the source of his fascination with ornament? The answer lies in the nature of the *The Autobiography of an Idea* itself. It was obviously crafted, as its title implies, as the gospel of a man who had come to see himself as a sort of messiah of American architecture. It is, therefore, more a piece of public relations than anything else. Thus, there was no room for either self criticism or any acknowledgment that the "Idea" was not entirely his own. Not only did Sullivan write his older brother Albert out of his life, he also avoided his failed marriage and the loss of his property to alcohol and debts, ending his account before either happened. It has been suggested that such omissions were the result of the decline of his own fortunes which left him self righteous, bitter and unforgiving, That does not explain, however, why as early as 1885, when he wrote his short autobiography for Andreas' *History of Chicago*, he created the myth of becoming Adler's partner two years before that actually happened. There he mentions working for Furness, Jenney and, "the famous Parisian architect," Vaudremer, and then lumps all his work experience for the next five years under, "faithful and practical study with leading firms," without ever mentioning his apprenticeship with Edelmann.[149] From the beginning of his career, Sullivan was busy reinventing himself as

---

[149] That Sullivan deliberately covered up his employment with Johnston & Edelmann is evident in the way he pretended to have almost no knowledge of Joseph S. Johnston in *The Autobiography*. Having decorated Johnston & Edelmann's Moody Tabernacle, he could hardly have avoided knowing precisely who Johnston was.

a prodigy. The true length and character of his years of apprenticeship with Edelmann and other relatively unknown architects had to be covered up as though it was something to be ashamed of. Due to the overwhelming debt he apparently felt he owed Edelmann, he could not bring himself to be quite as ruthless with him as he was with his brother. Nevertheless envy still seems to have clouded his memory.

Aside from these omissions and the somewhat "left handed" way Edelmann dealt with Sullivan's achievement in his *Pessimism of Modern Architecture*, we may never know the full depth of the feelings Sullivan and Edelmann ultimately had for each other. When writing his own autobiography in the 1960s, toward the end of his life, Edelmann's son summarized what he knew about the character of each of them:

> "What made Sullivan famous apart from his genius, was that he thought, dreamed and lived nothing but architecture; architecture was his whole life. My father, on the other hand, was involved in so many projects that I don't see how he designed as much as he did. A fair baritone and devotee of Wagnerian concerts, he was also an excellent amateur oarsman; he loved horses and both bred and raced them; and he was a sculptor, a painter, an anarchist and a Single Taxer."[150]

It is unlikely that after over sixty years such an assessment by a man who was only seven years old when his father died was merely the result of intuitive observation. Perhaps this is how Edelmann's wife had communicated her feelings and those of her husband to their son in the years following his death. Edelmann may not have become famous, but his son remembered him as something of a "Renaissance man." In comparison, how could Sullivan's poverty and the narrowness of his own life experience have left him anything but envious? It must be remembered, however, that if Sullivan had not stuck to his single minded "program in life," we would not have reason to remember either of them.

---

[150] Joseph Carter, Editor, *Labor Lobbyist, The Autobiography of John W. Edelmann*, p. 3.

PLATES

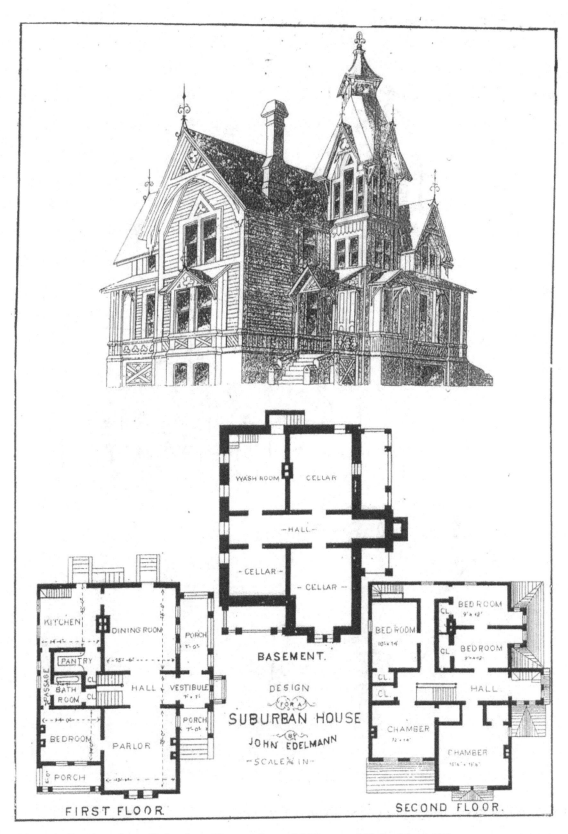

Plate 1. Design for a Suburban House from 1869 as published in 1872. *Paul E. Sprague*

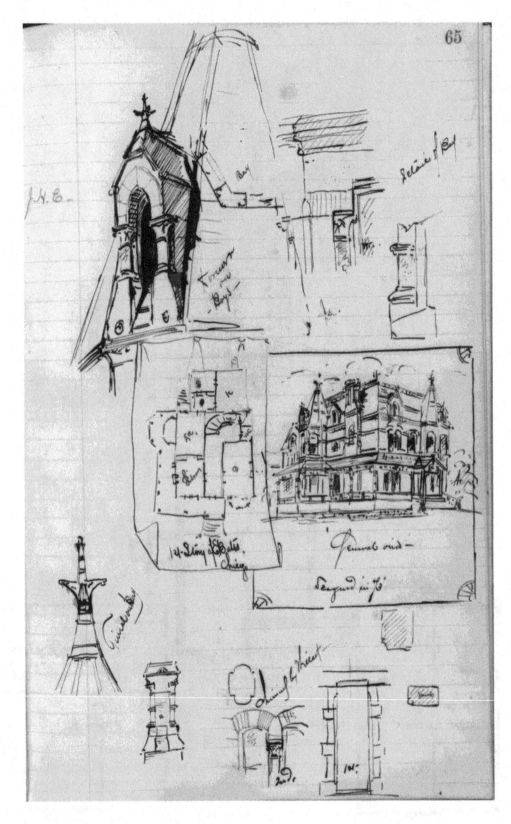

Plate 2. Bates Residence, Chicago, Sullivan's *Notebook* .

Avery Architectural and Fine Arts Library, Columbia University, New York.

CHICAGO CITY HALL COMPETITION.—PLAN SUBMITTED BY W. L. B. JENNY.

Plate 3. Competition design for City Hall and County Building, Chicago. *Chicago History Museum.*

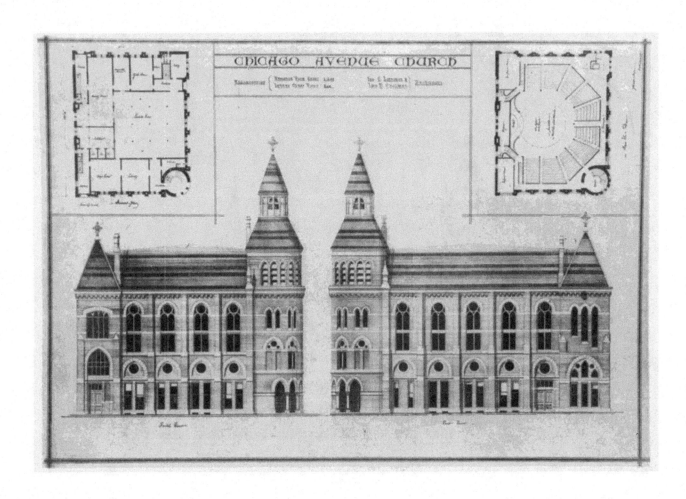

Plate 4. Moody Tabernacle, Chicago .

Avery Architectural and Fine Arts Library, Columbia University, New York.

Plate 5. Competition design for the Plymouth Congregational Church, Chicago.

Avery Architectural and Fine Arts Library, Columbia University, New York.

82

Plate 6. Study for a church in the Chicago suburb of Englewood, Sullivan's *Notebook.*

Avery Architectural and Fine Arts Library, Columbia University, New York.

Plate 7. Sinai Temple, Chicago. *Chicago History Museum.*

Plate 8a

Perspective for a two story school or court-house, Sullivan's *Notebook*. .

Avery Architectural and Fine Arts Library, Columbia University, New York.

8b.

Front Elevation for a cathedral for the 'Diocese of Cleveland' , Sulli-van's *Notebook*.

Avery Architectural and Fine Arts Library, Columbia University, New York.

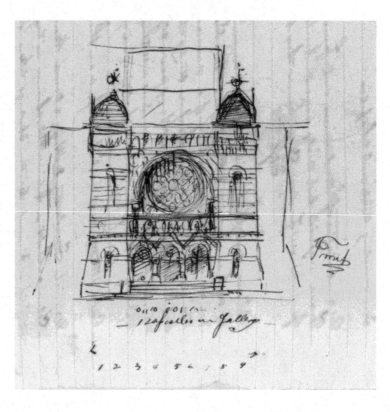

Plate 9. Central Music Hall, Chicago. *Ryerson & Burnham Libraries, Art Institute of Chicago*

Plate 10. Borden Residence, Chicago. *Chicago History Museum.*

Plate 11a

11b.

Strauss Residence, Chicago.Ca. 1920

Chicago History Museum

Strauss Residence, Chicago.Ca. 1960

Richard Nickel Committee, Chicago

Plate 12a. Kimball Building, Chicago. (After 1897 fire)

Chicago History Museum

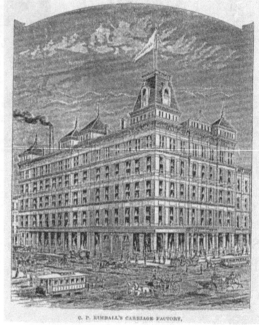

Plate 12b. Kimball Building, promotional woodcut.
Chicago: Illustrated and Discriptive

Chicago History Museum

Plate 13. Blackstone-Perkins Power Building, Cleveland. Seneca (now Third) St. Elevation.
Western Reserve Historical Society.

Plate 14. Wilshire Building, Cleveland.

Cleveland Public Library

Plate 15. Wilshire Building, Cleveland. Project for entrance.

Western Reserve Historical Society.

Plate 16. Stephens & Widlar Building, Cleveland.

Western Reserve Historical Society.

Plate 17. Gilman Building, Cleveland.

Western Reserve Historical Society.

Plate 18.   Edelmann's perspective of a Double House for Adler & Sullivan.

Richard Nickel Committee, Chicago

Plate 19. Knisely Store and Flat Building, Chicago. Upper and lower floors.

Richard Nickel Committee, Chicago.

Plate 20. Blumenfeld Flats, Chicago.

Richard Nickel Committee, Chicago

Plate 21. Frank Residence, Chicago.

Chicago Architectural Photographing Company.

Plate 22. McCormick and Selz Residences, Chicago.

Ryerson and Burnham Libraries, Art Institute of Chicago.

Plate 23. Barbe Residence, Chicago.

Chicago Architectual Photographing Company.

Plate 24. Two unit addition to the Ann Halsted Rowhouses, Chicago

Paul Petraitis

Plate 25, Duplex Flat Building, Chicago

Richard Nickel Committee, Chicago.

Plate 26. Edelmann's perspective of the Eighth Avenue front of The Gospel Tabernacle, New York.

Christian and Missionary Alliance

Plate 27. Riverside Baptist Church, New York.

Library of Congress

Plate 28. Branford High School, Branford, CT.

Branford Historical Society.

Plate 29. Rothschild Store, Chicago.

Ryerson and Burnham Libraries, Art Institute of Chicago.

Plate 30. Maxwell Store, Chicago.

Ryerson and Burnham Libraries, Art Institute of Chicago.

Plate 31. Academy of Music, Kalamazoo, MI.

Kalamazoo Valley Museum.

Plate 32. Wineman Residence, Chicago.

Ryerson and Burnham Libraries, Art Institute of Chicago.

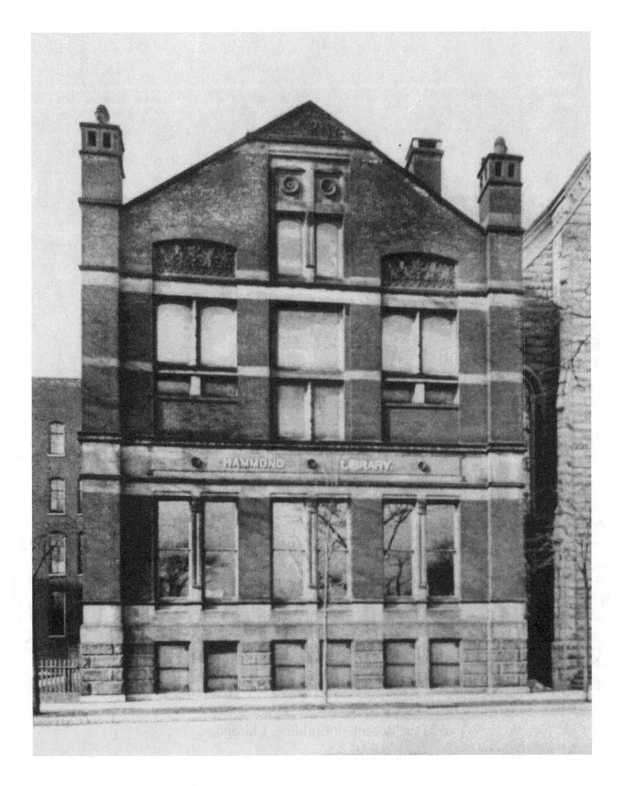

Plate 33. Hammond Library, Chicago.

Richard Nickel Committee, Chicago.

Plate 34. Nevada Hotel part of the Rosenfeld Building, Chicago.

Ryerson and Burnham Libraries, Art Institute of Chicago.

Plate 35. Edelmann's perspective of the Troescher Building, Chicago.

Ryerson and Burnham Libraries, Art Institute of Chicago.

a.

b.

c.

Plate 36. St. James Episcopal Church, Chicago. a. Entrance hinge

b. Door Casing   c. Organ Loft detail

Charles E. Gregersen

Plate 37. Drawing for "Spandrel-synagogue."

Avery Architectural and Fine Arts Library, Columbia University, New York.

Plate 38a. Borden Residence, Chicago. Exterior detail of north wall.

Richard Nickel Committee, Chicago.

38b. Kimball Building, Chicago. Spandrel detail.

Charles E. Gregersen

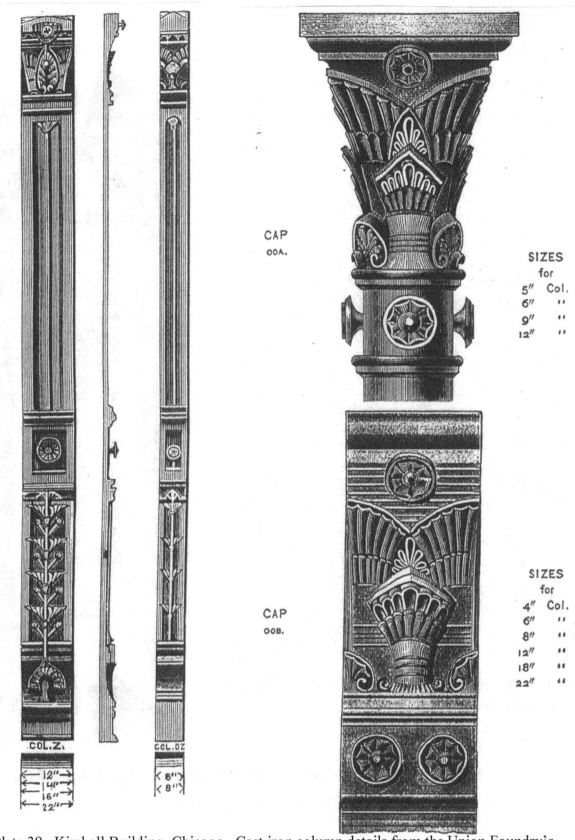

Plate 39. Kimball Building, Chicago. Cast iron column details from the Union Foundry's *Manual.*

Chicago History Museum.

Plate 40a. Ornament from Christopher Dresser's *Principles of Decorative Design*,

Plate 40b. Strauss Residence, Chicago. Exterior detail.

Richard Nickel Committee, Chicago.

Plate 41a. Blackstone Building, Cleveland.
Bust and lintel over entrance.
Cleveland Public Library.

Plate 41b. Interior spandrel.
Western Reserve Historical Society.
Martin Linsey photo

Plate 42a. Guy Perkins' Alphabet Book.
Carved wood cover.

Western Reserve Historical Society.

Plate 42b. Guy Perkins' Alphabet Book.
Letter Z.

Western Reserve Historical Society.

Plate 43a. Wilshire Building, Cleveland. Top floor detail.

Cleveland Public Library.

Plate 43b. Gilman Building, Cleveland. Ornament over corner entrance.

Richard Nickel Committee, Chicago.

Plate 44a. Gilman Building, Cleveland.
Inverted view of metal bracket at second floor.
Richard Nickel Committee, Chicago.

Plate 44b. Duplex, Chicago. Pediment detail.
Richard Nickel Committee, Chicago.

Plate 45. Interior plaster ceiling escutcheon from one of the Ann Halsted Rowhouses, Chicago.

Charles E. Gregersen

CATALOG OF THE KNOWN
ARCHITECTURAL WORKS OF JOHN EDELMANN

1869 probably for Alexander Koehler Architect, Cleveland

1. "Country house designed in 1869," published under Edelmann's name in 1872 but may never have been built.

1872 for Burling & Adler Architects, Chicago

2. Eli Bates Residence, no longer extant, 1304 N. Dearborn Street, Chicago.

1873 for Burling & Adler Architects, Chicago

3. First Congregational Church, no longer extant, northeast corner of Kenilworth Avenue and Lake Street, Oak Park, Illinois.

1873 for William Le Baron Jenney Architect, Chicago

4. Unsuccessful competition design for a proposed City Hall and County Building, Chicago.

1873 for Joseph S. Johnston, Architect, Chicago

5. Moody Tabernacle, no longer extant, northwest corner of LaSalle Street and Chicago Avenue, Chicago.

1874, Johnston & Edelmann, Architects, Chicago

6. Unsuccessful competition design for the Plymouth Congregational Church, Chicago.

1875, Johnston & Edelmann, Architects, Chicago

7. St. James Episcopal Church (now Cathedral) extant, southeast corner of Wabash Avenue and Huron Street, Chicago. Design consultant to Burling & Adler, Architects to rebuild that part of the front destroyed in the 1871 fire and undertake the, "refitting," of the interior of the shell left by the work of Clarke & Faulkner, Architects when their work was suspended in 1873.
8. Sinai Temple, no longer extant, southwest corner of 21st Street and Indiana Avenue, Chicago. Design consultant to Dankmar Adler for Burling & Adler, Architects.
9. "Study," for a church in the Chicago suburb of Englewood.
10. Design for a cathedral for the, "Diocese of Cleveland."

1876, Johnston & Edelmann, Architects, Chicago

11. Perspective for a small two story public building, most likely a school.
12. Central Music Hall, no longer extant, southeast corner of State and Randolph streets, Chicago. Design consultant to Dankmar Adler for Burling & Adler (1876 and 1878) and Dankmar Adler, Architect (1879). Building begun in 1879 by Dankmar Adler, Architect.

1877 for Alexander Koehler Architect, Cleveland

13. Central School, New Philadelphia, Ohio, no longer extant, probably serving only as a construction superintendent.

1880 for Dankmar Adler Architect, Chicago

14. Grand Opera House, no longer extant, 119 N. Clark Street, Chicago.
15. John Borden Residence, no longer extant, 3949 S. Lake Park Avenue in the suburb of Hyde Park, now part of Chicago.

1880 John H. Edelmann Architect, Chicago

16. Leopold Strauss Residence, no longer extant, 1848 S. Michigan Avenue, Chicago
17. C. P, Kimball Carriage Co. Building, no longer extant, northwest corner of Harrison Street and Wabash Avenue, Chicago. Design consultant to Cyrus P. Thomas, Architect,

1881 for Coburn and Barnum, Architects, Cleveland

18. Climax Building, no longer extant, 1440-1454 West Third Street, Cleveland, construction superintendent only.
19. Ornamental treatment of the Blackstone—Perkins Power Building, no longer extant, 1420-34 West Third Street (Blackstone front), 321 Frankfort Street (Perkins Power front), Cleveland.
20. Canopy over the casket of President James A. Garfield, the Public Square, Cleveland, removed after the funeral was over.

1882 John H. Edelmann, Architect, Cleveland

21. Wilshire Building, no longer extant, 328-408 Superior Street, Cleveland.
22. Stephens & Widlar Building (also known as the Kingsley Building) no longer extant, 321-331 St. Clair Street, Cleveland.
23. The Gilman Building (later Herron Building) extant, greatly altered, facade has been covered since the 1960s by a metal skin, 1350-64 West Third Street and 307 St. Clair Street, Cleveland.

1883-85 for Adler & Sullivan, Architects, Chicago

24. Unexecuted design for a Double House at 2441-45 S. Wabash Avenue, Chicago.
25. Knisely Store and Flats, no longer extant, 2147 W. Lake Street, Chicago.
26. Kaufmann Store and Flats, extant, 2310 N. Lincoln Avenue, Chicago.
27. Solomon Blumenfeld Flats, no longer extant, 8 W. Chicago Ave., Chicago.
28. Louis E. Frank Residence, no longer extant, 3219 S. Michigan Avenue, Chicago.
29. Martin Barbe Residence, no longer extant, 3157 S. Prairie Avenue, Chicago.
30. Anna McCormick Residence, no longer extant, 1715 S. Michigan Avenue, Chicago.
31. Ornamental details on several other designs of the firm (see page 45).

1883-84 for S. S. Beman, Architect, Chicago

32. Iron staircases and elevator cages of the Pullman Building, no longer extant, southwest corner of Michigan Avenue and Adams Street, Chicago.

1885-87, John H. Edelmann, Architect, Chicago

33. Two unit addition to the Ann Halsted Rowhouses, 1832-34 N. Lincoln Park West, Chicago
34. Duplex apartment building, no longer extant, location unknown, Chicago.

1887-90, Edelmann & Smith, Architects, New York

35. Riverside Baptist Church, no longer extant replaced in 1916 on the site by the present Central Baptist Church, southeast corner 92nd Street and 10th (now Amsterdam) Avenue, New York City.
36. The Gospel Tabernacle, greatly altered, front replaced in 1925 when a sixth floor was added to the height of the original building, east side of Eighth Avenue between 43rd and 44th Streets, New York

1891-94, for Alfred Zucker, Architect, New York

37. Decker Building, extant, 33 Union Square, New York.
38. Hotel Majestic interiors, no longer extant, southwest corner 72nd Street and Central Park West, New York.

1893-94, John H. Edelmann, Architect, New York

39. Residence for Mr. and Mrs. John H. Edelmann, extant, front greatly altered, 30 Alpine Place, North Arlington (now Kearney) New Jersey.
40. Branford High School, no longer extant, Laurel Street, Branford, Connecticut.